By the same Author

LANDMARKS IN THE STORY OF CHRISTIANITY
THE STUDY OF THE GOSPELS
THE ACTS OF THE APOSTLES
A CRITICAL INTRODUCTION TO THE GOSPELS
THE SYNOPTIC GOSPELS
THE GOSPEL AND LETTERS OF JOHN
WHO'S WHO IN THE GOSPELS
THE GOSPEL OF MARK
THE CHURCH IN THE NEW TESTAMENT
THE GOSPEL OF MATTHEW
THE GOSPEL OF LUKE
THE FOURTH GOSPEL – AN INTRODUCTION

THE LIFE OF CHRIST

NOTES ON THE NARRATIVE AND TEACHING IN THE GOSPELS

By

H. A. GUY, B.D., B.A.

Macmillan Education

First Edition 1951
Reprinted 1953 (twice), 1955, 1957, 1959, 1961, 1964, 1966, 1969, 1971, 1972, 1974, 1976, 1979

Published by
MACMILLAN EDUCATION LIMITED
Houndmills Basingstoke Hampshire RG21 2XS
and London
Associated companies in Delhi Dublin
Hong Kong Johannesburg Lagos Melbourne
New York Singapore and Tokyo

ISBN 0 333 00205 9

Printed in Hong Kong by
Wing King Tong Co Ltd

FOREWORD

By the Rev. F. B. Clogg, M.A., B.D., Professor of New Testament Language and Literature in the University of London.

An important part of the Religious Knowledge paper in the new General Certificate of Education is "The Life and Teaching of Christ". The text-book is of course the Gospels themselves, which have been the source of innumerable commentaries written for widely different types of readers. Most teachers of this subject, while they study as many as they can of the commentaries and other books written about the Gospels, will welcome a book written by one who, through his own experience, knows the sort of help which many of them need.

Most books on the Life and Teaching of Christ combine elements from the Fourth Gospel with the story of the ministry in the Synoptic Gospels. The important differences between the Fourth Gospel and the Synoptic Gospels make it desirable to have a text-book which treats these two main sources separately. Hitherto no suitable book has been obtainable. My friend and former pupil, Mr. H. A. Guy, is well qualified academically and from practical experience to write such a text-book. I believe his book will be of great value to those teachers who have not been able to specialize in this subject. Even those who have specialized will be grateful for the guidance which it offers. It is in no sense a substitute for the Gospels themselves but a book which, if rightly used, will give both teachers and taught a more lively appreciation of the significance of what the Gospels tell us of the Life and Teaching of Christ. It will be of value to those who are teaching the subject not only with an examination in view, but who are using one or other of the excellent Agreed Syllabuses in Religious Instruction.

I have often been asked by teachers to recommend a text-book. I commend this as the sort of book for which they have been seeking.

F. B. Clogg.

CONTENTS

THE USE OF THIS BOOK

This book is intended for two types of readers:

(i) Those who wish to make a study of the life and teaching of Christ privately or who wish to have at hand a book for convenient reference to any particular passage. It may thus prove of use to students of all ages, to teachers and to preachers and to any who wish to know more of the story which is the foundation of Christianity.

(ii) Candidates for examinations on the narrative and teaching in the Gospels. These students should make certain, from the regulations and syllabus of their examination, which part or parts they are expected to know.

(*a*) If they are to read only one of the Gospels, they should refer to the table of sections or the index of passages, to select those sections which deal with this particular Gospel.

(*b*) If their subject is 'The Life and Teaching of Jesus, as recorded in the Synoptic Gospels' *only Part I* should be studied now. Experience shows that to read the Fourth Gospel narratives at the same time causes confusion in the mind of the student, which is reflected in answers in the examination room.

(*c*) If their syllabus includes the narrative portions of the Fourth Gospel, Part II should be studied as well.

For all students, the introduction, dealing with the writing of the Gospels and the background of the New Testament, is essential. This may be read either before or after the Gospel passages have been studied.

The actual matter in the Gospels is not printed here. This is of set purpose. The text-book is the New Testament and this book is not intended to take the place of that. It is essential that the New Testament itself should be read and that the student should be able to 'find his way about' the Gospels. The notes in each section are intended only as a guide to a fuller understanding of the contents of the Gospels. It is assumed in these that the English Revised Version of 1881 is being used, but the book may be employed with any English translation of the New Testament. For consulting parallel passages it would be a convenience to have two or three copies.

The matter in the Synoptic Gospels is divided into a hundred and seventy-three sections. This is for purposes of comparison and reference. At the head of each section there are references to all the places where the incident or teaching is to be found. If there is more than one account, the passage which should be read first, if that is desirable, is underlined. Differences which occur in the parallel accounts in the other Gospels are dealt with in the notes and should be looked up.

The advantage of this arrangement is that we can gain a clear idea of each section, in comparative isolation from other matter with which it might be confused. The danger is that we may tend to think of the Gospels as consisting of a number of separate sections or isolated fragments. To counteract this, the student is strongly advised to read through the Gospels first—preferably in the order Mark, Luke, Matthew—or the particular Gospel, if he is studying only one. He will then gain a general impression of the course of the story of Jesus and the contents of his teaching. Then he can turn to the separate sections here, for light on particular passages. After concluding his study he will do well to read the Gospels once again, bearing in mind the notes and suggestions he has found here.

The Revised Standard Version is now in general use as the basic text for examinations. It is much the same as the Revised Version, without its archaisms. Students may also find help from the New English Bible.

INTRODUCTION

The Making of the Gospels

The main part of this book deals with the matter found in the first three Gospels. These are grouped together as the Synoptic Gospels. This is from two Greek words meaning 'seen together' and refers to the fact that parallel passages can be seen thus in a 'Synopsis', when the three accounts are placed side by side.[1] It also means that the three writers look at the life of Jesus from the same 'synoptic' point of view. The three are thus distinguished from the Fourth Gospel, which gives an account differing in chronology, in the presentation of the events narrated, in the style of Jesus' teaching and in the place of most of his public work.

The question of the relationship between the first three Gospels is called the Synoptic Problem. There are many books which deal with this in detail. All that can be given here is a summary of the conclusions which the great majority of Protestant scholars throughout the world have reached:

(i) Before the composition of the written Gospels, stories about Jesus and sayings of his were told orally by the Christians. People in the East have extraordinarily good memories and this was and still is a common method of passing on information and teaching. These stories circulated in the Church mainly as separate units, often detached from particulars of time or place.

(ii) These stories have been classified according to their contents and form.

[1] A convenient synopsis in English is A. Huck: *Gospel Parallels*

(*a*) Some stories end with a pronouncement of Jesus and were remembered for the sake of the saying. See, for example, the account of Jesus and the outcasts (Section 22), Jesus and the Sabbath (24), Jesus' true family (29), Jesus and the children (94), the rich man (95), the question of tribute (140), the question of the inheritance (111), the coming of the Kingdom of God (128).

(*b*) Stories which told of Jesus' miracles and healing-acts, to illustrate his power and authority. See, for example, the leper (20), the Gerasene madman (66), the daughter of Jairus (67), the epileptic boy (85), the widow's son (62).

(*c*) Stories about Jesus or about people who lived with him were told as short biographical sketches. See, for example, Jesus' boyhood (10), the baptism and temptation (13 and 14), the visit to Nazareth (70), Caesarea Philippi (83), the transfiguration (84). Sketches of other people include: the call of the disciples (15), the sinful woman (63), Martha and Mary (104), the meeting with Zacchaeus (132).

(*d*) Sayings of Jesus were told similarly. Probably the sayings and parables were collected together and written down before the stories.

(iii) These separate units were gathered together by the early Christians and were used by the writers of our Gospels. They connected the stories by links consisting of editorial notes and sometimes grouped the sayings to form a connected discourse. The writers of our Gospels were thus not biographers or authors in the modern sense, but were mainly compilers and editors, selecting their material in accordance with their purpose.

The work of examining the early traditions in the forms which they took, before they were written down, is called Form-Criticism or Form-History. This is to be distinguished from Source-Criticism, the study of the written documents used by the evangelists, with which the following paragraphs deal.

(iv) We find that the first three of our written Gospels are very similar in many ways—in the general order of events and, in parallel passages, often in the very wording. From a close study of the three books and of every such passage, it has been concluded that the first to be written was the Gospel of Mark. Ninety-five per cent of Mark's matter is found in Matthew, while at least fifty-five per cent of Mark is given also in Luke. For typical passages see the healing of the paralytic (Section 21), the call of Levi (22), Jairus' daughter (67), the question of Jesus' authority (137).

Mark's book was thus the first attempt to make a connected account of the early stories and sayings of Jesus. This Gospel was used by the other two writers and incorporated in their work. This was quite a common practice in the first century.

(v) This accounts for over half of Matthew and over a third of Luke. These two writers have in addition other passages where they are very similar. Here we conclude that they used another document besides Mark, a collection of Jesus' teaching, which is now lost. This document is called Q (from the German word *Quelle*, meaning source). For typical Q matter see the teaching of John the Baptist (Section 12), the mote and the beam (55), the two foundations (60), would-be followers (100).

This accounts for about a half of the non-Markan matter in Matthew and just under a third of the non-Markan matter in Luke.

(vi) There is matter found only in Matthew. This consists mainly of teaching of Jesus and is called for convenience M. Matter found only in Luke consists of teaching and narratives and is called L.

The following diagram (adapted from B. H. Streeter's *The Four Gospels*) makes clear the relationship between the Gospels.

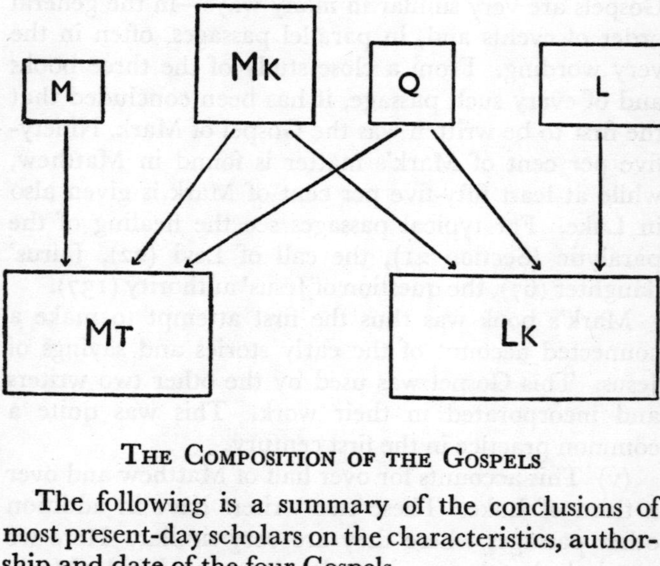

THE COMPOSITION OF THE GOSPELS

The following is a summary of the conclusions of most present-day scholars on the characteristics, authorship and date of the four Gospels.

MARK

(*a*) The style of Mark's Gospel is a vivid one. There is an impression of speed and urgency. The language, in the original Greek, is rugged and sometimes harsh. Transition from one paragraph to another is often abrupt.

The aim of the writer was to present 'the good news of Jesus Christ' (1: 1). Mark was writing for those within the Christian Church who desired to have a written record of familiar matters. His first readers were probably Gentiles, for he takes the trouble to explain references to Jewish customs and words. He is particularly interested in the deeds of Jesus. He portrays him as a man of authority and action and as the Messiah and Servant of God. There are not many sections of the *teaching* of Jesus in Mark.

(*b*) The book was probably written by John Mark, who is mentioned in Acts 12: 12, 12: 25, 13: 5, 13: 13, 15: 37–39; Colossians 4: 10; Philemon verse 24; 2 Timothy 4: 11. According to tradition, Mark relied on the reminiscences of Peter, and there are places where we think we can see Peter behind the narrative. He probably used also written accounts of some of the incidents and one collection or more of Jesus' sayings.

(*c*) The usual date assigned to Mark is the sixties of the first century. Some think it was written when the Christians in Rome were being persecuted by the emperor Nero (A.D. 64–65). Some scholars, however, date it about the time of the fall of Jerusalem in A.D. 70.

MATTHEW

(*a*) This is a typically Jewish Gospel. There is a great interest in the Old Testament, from which many quotations are given (especially from the prophets) and other Jewish features. Matthew wrote to portray Jesus as the Son of David, the Jewish Messiah. In his teaching Jesus is shown as the new Lawgiver. His sayings are arranged in five discourses or books. Matthew has also a greater interest than the other Synoptic writers in eschatology (teaching about the Last Things) and in the miraculous element in the story. He wrote for the Christian Church and sought to consolidate its fellowship.

(*b*) The author was a Jewish Christian, with an outlook like that of the scribes. He was not an apostle or eye-witness of the life of Jesus, for the basis of his book is Mark's Gospel, not personal reminiscences, and his own special matter is sometimes historically improbable. The book was attributed to Matthew the apostle probably because of the words of an early second-century writer (Papias, bishop of Hierapolis in Asia Minor), who said that Matthew wrote 'the sayings' in Aramaic. This (whatever it was) may have been used by the author of our Gospel of Matthew, but his book is really a revised edition of Mark, with matter from Q and M added.

(*c*) The book is generally dated about A.D. 85 or later, and the place was possibly Antioch in Syria or further east, in northern Assyria.

LUKE

(*a*) This is the most literary of the Gospels. It is written in good Greek style and is perhaps the first attempt to write a proper biography of Jesus. It was penned, together with the Acts of the Apostles, for a Roman official, Theophilus (Luke 1 : 1–4 and Acts 1 : 1). The writer's approach to the story of Jesus is that of a Gentile. He presents him as the universal Christ. He shows great interest in outcast people (sinners, tax-collectors, Samaritans), in the work of women, in the subject of prayer and in Jesus' teaching about the Spirit.

(*b*) The author is probably to be identified with Luke, who is mentioned in Colossians 4: 14; Philemon verse 24; 2 Timothy 4: 11. From these references we gather that he was a doctor, a companion of Paul and a Gentile. There are also passages in Acts where the writer uses the first person plural. These 'we-passages' tell us that the author accompanied Paul on journeys in Greece and later to Rome.

(*c*) Some think that Luke wrote first a book or a draft of a book, with material from Q and L. This would be about A.D. 58. Later he incorporated Markan matter, to complete his account. The usual date assigned to the completed Gospel (and Acts) is A.D. 75–80.

JOHN

(*a*) In many ways this is very different from the Synoptics. The subject matter has only five narratives in common with the other Gospels, excluding the Passion story; it is difficult, if not impossible, to fit into the Synoptic account the special matter in this Gospel. Jesus here speaks in long discourses and in allegories, instead of pithy sayings and parables. The book is written in the same Greek style, which appears to be that of the author himself. The teaching given seems in many places to represent the developed theology of the Church towards the end of the first century.

There are, however, points of contact with the Synoptic story and the usual conclusion is that the writer knew and used Mark and Luke. He wrote to reinterpret the familiar story. He gave a new presentation to almost everything he touched, whether narrative or the teaching of Jesus. His primary aim seems to have been that his readers might 'believe' and 'have eternal life' (20: 31). But he had also in mind some Jewish opponents of the Church and certain false views of Christianity. He was a philosopher and a theologian and told his story in terms of current Greek thought.

(*b*) The traditional view was that the author was the apostle John, who was thought to be referring to himself as 'the disciple whom Jesus loved'. Few New

Testament scholars of repute now assign the book to the apostle. Some think it was written by the man who penned the short books in the New Testament known as 2 and 3 John, who calls himself 'The Elder'. This may have been an elder or presbyter of Ephesus named John, a later leader in the Church. If the 'beloved disciple' ('Jesus' favourite disciple', as Moffatt translates) was intended to be John, his figure was probably idealized by the writer, so that in the book he stands for the true disciple of Jesus.

The writer was acquainted with educated Jewish and Greek thought, especially with the type of philosophy associated with Alexandria. He was probably a Hellenistic Jew, although acquainted with Palestine and Jerusalem.

(*c*) The usual date assigned to the Gospel is A.D. 95–105.

The Background of the Life of Jesus

(*a*) *The historical background of the Gospels*

In order to understand and to be able to appreciate any great man of history, we must know something of the people among whom he lived and from whom he came —not only their situation in his own time but their history for a long period before. This is no less true of Jesus.

Jesus was a Jew and lived in Palestine. That statement supplies at once the key to much that is found in the Gospels. The story of his people—the Hebrews— is told in the Old Testament. This is the historical background of the New Testament. That history must be studied in the Old Testament itself and in the Apocrypha, which tells of the events between the Old Testament and the New. There are numerous books available today for those who wish to read about this. The following list of nine historical periods of Hebrew history may be useful:

Period I	The Patriarchal Age (from about 1700 B.C.)
II	The Exodus from Egypt (about 1200 or 1400 B.C.)
III	The Settlement in Canaan
IV	The Monarchy (from 1030 B.C.)
V	The divided Kingdom (930–722 B.C.)
VI	The Southern Kingdom alone (722–586 B.C.)
VII	The Exile in Babylon (586 B.C. onwards)
VIII	The Return from Exile (538 B.C. onwards)
IX	Between the Old Testament and the New (from 400 B.C.).

More important even than the facts of their history is the religion of the Hebrews. This progressed, in the course of hundreds of years, until the height of their thought about God and man was reached in the time of the Exile.

Both the history and the religion are taken for granted in the New Testament. The first disciples were Jews, as were also the authors of the Gospels, with the exception of Luke. There are many references to Old Testament books in them, some direct and others incidental. The climax of Old Testament religion was the belief in one God, who desired righteousness and love from his worshippers. This is called ethical monotheism and was the result of the teaching of the prophets. This position could be taken for granted by Jesus. It was assumed both by himself and by his hearers that there was but one God and that he asked for a high standard of conduct from men. Jesus was able to use this as a foundation, on which to raise the structure of his own teaching.

(*b*) *The religious situation at the time of Jesus*

The Jews in the Roman Empire were allowed to keep their own religious beliefs and practices. The Romans were generally tolerant in such matters, provided the religious enthusiasm of subject peoples did not lead to public disturbance or attempts to revolt.

Judaism by the time of the first century A.D. had become one of the chief legalistic religions of the world. This means that its observance consisted mainly in certain religious duties. The man who observed these and carried out the Law was a pious man, blessed by God and respected by his fellows. The man who neglected them was an outcast, from both human and divine society.

For strict Jews there were certain private or semi-public observances. These included fasting—twice a week was the usual practice—almsgiving, which included the paying of tithes to the priests and the giving of charity to beggars, and prayer, at set hours of the day, either in private or in the company of other people.

There was also worship. The usual place was the synagogue, where services were held not only every Sabbath but during the week as well. The name simply means a gathering or assembly, and synagogues probably started during the Exile in Babylon, when sacrificial worship was impossible owing to the destruction of the Temple at Jerusalem. By the first century there were numerous synagogues, wherever Jews lived, in Palestine or elsewhere. The building was a simple one, square in shape. There was no altar, but a platform, a reading-desk and a cupboard or curtained-off place where the rolls of the Old Testament books were kept. The service also was simple—prayers, the chanting of Psalms, readings from the Law and the Prophets, the recitation of Hebrew passages and an address, often followed by a discussion. The service was conducted by a Rabbi or by one of the elders (or rulers) of the synagogue—a committee of prominent local men who managed the affairs of the synagogue.

Quite distinct from this was the Temple, in Jerusalem. The Temple in Jesus' time was the third. The first was Solomon's, which had been destroyed by the Babylonians when they took Jerusalem in 586 B.C. The second had been built in 520 B.C. after the return of the Jews from Exile. The third had been started by Herod the Great in 20 B.C. He did not complete it, and it was indeed not finished until A.D. 65, five years before it was destroyed by the Romans. The Temple building itself was entered only by the priests, and the innermost shrine, the Holy of Holies, was entered only by the High Priest and by him only on one day in the year, the Day of Atonement. Surrounding the Temple was a Court of the Priests, where there were altars on which the priests offered sacrifice. Outside this were two courts into which only Jews were allowed to go—the inner Court of the Men of Israel, where only men were permitted, and the Court of the Women, into which any Jews might go. Surrounding these courts was the Court of the Gentiles, where anyone was allowed, and this had around it covered porticos.

The Temple was a place for sacrifice, not a place of congregational worship like the synagogue. It was associated in particular with the great religious festivals, such as the Passover, Pentecost and Tabernacles. Jews from all over the Roman world would visit Jerusalem then, as a religious duty and joy.

The Jews who wished to be particularly strict in their

religion belonged to one of the religious parties. These must not be thought of as separate 'denominations', for all acknowledged the same Law, worshipped in the synagogues and sacrificed in the Temple. But there was often strife between them because of their differences in outlook.

The PHARISEES are the best-known. The name means 'separate' and was probably adopted to stress the differences between Jews and Gentiles. Unfortunately the Pharisees themselves became 'separate' from the majority of their fellow-Jews, who were not so strict as they were.

Many of the Pharisees were middle-class laymen—business men and shopkeepers. Their great interest was in the Law and the business of the synagogue. They believed fervently in the Old Testament and accepted also the 'oral traditions'—amplifications and interpretations of the Law which had been made by scribes and Rabbis of former generations. They believed in a future resurrection of dead people, after a stay in Hades; after this would come a Judgment by God. They believed that God himself would set up his Kingdom. Their task was to help by observing the Law. They held to the hope of a Messiah, who would be God's agent in setting up and ruling his Kingdom. They disliked the rule of the Romans, but took no steps to revolt against it. They held that when God was satisfied with the nation of Israel, when they kept his Law perfectly, he himself would deliver them.

No doubt many of the Pharisees were sincere worshippers of God, who were trying to please him. Such a one was Saul of Tarsus. But their insistence on the keeping of the Law and the traditions led them to be very stern towards people who did not come up to their own high standard. They despised the common people and held themselves aloof from all disreputable folk and 'outcasts'.

The SADDUCEES were possibly called after Zadok, a priest of Solomon's time. Their members were mostly priests and aristocrats from noble Jewish families. They accepted the written Law but rejected the oral traditions of the Pharisees. Consequently they did not believe in a future resurrection or a Messiah. They owed the security of their position to the Romans, so they supported the conqueror's rule.

In the Gospels we find the Pharisees opposing Jesus, in Galilee. It was not until he came to Jerusalem that the priests and Sadducees began to take notice of him. In the Acts the Sadducees are the enemies of the disciples in Jerusalem.

The ZEALOTS were, as their name implies, an extreme religious and political party. They were the fanatical nationalists and developed from a movement started by Judas of Galilee, who rose against a Roman census in A.D. 6 (see Acts 5: 37). They were responsible for the rebellion of A.D. 65–70, which resulted in the destruction of the Temple and the end of the Jewish nation. They believed that God's Kingdom could be set up on earth by force.

The SCRIBES were not a separate religious party, but were a professional class. Originally they were the men who copied the manuscripts of the Old Testament books. From their acquaintance with these writings they became the acknowledged teachers and interpreters of the Law. Most of them probably belonged to the Pharisee party, but some were Sadducees.

Most of the ordinary people of Palestine did not ally themselves with any of these parties or classes. They had not the leisure to study the Law minutely, to apply it diligently and exactly, and so did not join the Pharisees. They were not priests, so would not become Sadducees. They disliked the Romans but were not prepared to rise in active revolt, so they were not Zealots. 'Sheep without a shepherd' well describes them. These were the people to whom Jesus appealed.

(*c*) *The political situation*

The overlords of Palestine in the first century were the Romans. In 63 B.C. Pompey had entered Palestine with his army and captured Jerusalem. The country became part of the Roman Empire and was incorporated in the province of Syria.

The Romans often allowed native kings or chiefs to have power over their own territories. Herod the Great (whose family were originally not Jews) was permitted, from 37 B.C., to call himself king of the Jews. He was an able but cruel ruler. He worked with the Romans and was frequently hated by the Jews. He began the new Temple mentioned in the previous section.

On the death of Herod, in 4 B.C., his kingdom was split up among three of his sons. Herod Archelaus was given the southern portion, Judea and Idumea. In A.D. 6 he was deposed by the Romans, because of the complaints of the people, and a Roman procurator was appointed to look after this territory. The fifth procurator was Pontius Pilate, from A.D. 26–36. Herod Philip was given Iturea, north-east of the Jordan. He died in A.D. 34. Herod Antipas was given Galilee, in the north, and Perea, east of the Jordan valley. He married the daughter of the king of Damascus but, attracted by Herodias, the wife of a half-brother, he divorced his own wife and married her.

In A.D. 39 he asked the Romans for the title of king (his own official title was tetrarch, or ruler of a fourth part); he was deposed and sent into exile by the Romans.

The three parts into which the territory of the Jews was divided in the time of Jesus are shown on the map on page 16. Judea included also the district of Samaria. This was inhabited by descendants of Assyrian colonists, who had been imported into the northern kingdom when Samaria fell to the Assyrians in 722 B.C. They had mingled with the Israelites who remained after the leading people had been taken to Assyria. The Samaritans adopted the worship of Yahweh, the Hebrew God, and on the return of the Jewish exiles from Babylon to Judea they offered to help in rebuilding the Temple at Jerusalem (520 B.C.). Their help was refused, so for a long time they tried to hinder the fortification and building of the city. Eventually they built their own rival Temple on Mount Gerizim in Samaria. This was destroyed by a Jewish king in 110 B.C. There was great bitterness between Jews and Samaritans, and they generally avoided one another as much as possible.

In A.D. 39 Herod Agrippa I, grandson of Herod the Great, was made king of Judea (see Acts 12: 1–2 and 12: 20–23). On his death in A.D. 44, he was succeeded by his son, Herod Agrippa II (Acts 25: 13–27), who was the last of the Jewish kings. In A.D. 65 a revolt against the Romans broke out in Galilee. This spread and became a general rebellion. The Romans sent the general Vespasian to put it down, and when he went to Rome to be Emperor in A.D. 69 his son Titus carried on the war. In A.D. 70 he captured Jerusalem, after a terrible siege, and destroyed the city and the Temple.

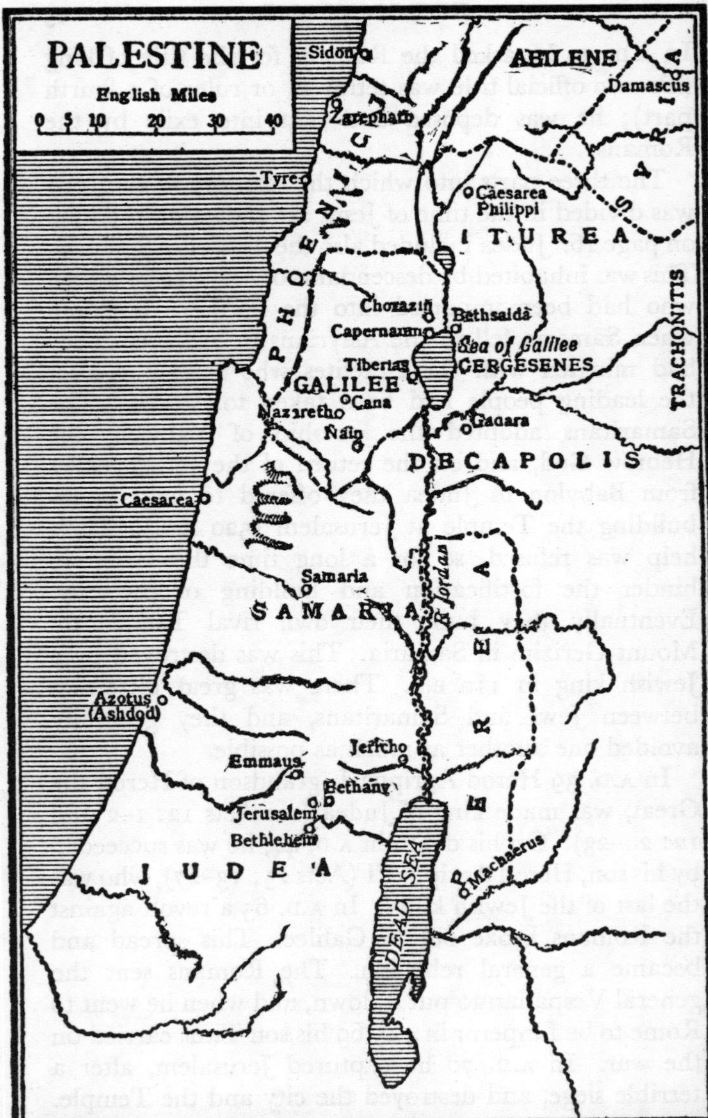

EMERY WALKER LTD.

PART I

The Life and Teaching of Jesus, according to the Synoptic Gospels

LIST OF SECTIONS

I. *JESUS' BIRTH AND BOYHOOD*

	Matthew	*Mark*	*Luke*
(*a*) *Matthew's account:*			
1. The annunciation of the birth of Jesus . .	1: 18–25		
2. The birth of Jesus. Visit of the Magi. Stay in Egypt and settlement at Nazareth . .	2: 1–23		
(*b*) *Luke's account:*			
3. The prologue to Luke's Gospel . . .			1: 1–4
4. The annunciation of the birth of John the Baptist . . .			1: 5–25
5. The annunciation of the birth of Jesus . .			1: 26–38
6. The meeting of Mary and Elizabeth . .			1: 39–56
7. The birth of John the Baptist . . .			1: 57–80
8. The birth of Jesus. The visit of the shepherds			2: 1–20
9. The presentation in the Temple. Return to Nazareth . .			2: 21–40
10. The boyhood of Jesus .			2: 41–52
General note on the birth stories			
(*c*) *Jesus' family:*			
11. The genealogies . .	1: 1–17		3: 23–38

II. THE WORK OF JESUS IN GALILEE

	Matthew	*Mark*	*Luke*
(*a*) *The preaching of John the Baptist:*			
12. The message of John .	3: 1–12	1: 1–8	3: 1–20
13. The baptism of Jesus by John . . .	3: 13–17	1: 9–11	3: 21–22
14. The temptations of Jesus	4: 1–11	1: 12–13	4: 1–13
(*b*) *Jesus' preaching and healing:*			
15. Jesus' return to Galilee. The call of four disciples . . .	4: 12–22	1: 14–20	4: 14–15
16. The call of Peter and the catch of fish .			5: 1–11
17. Jesus in the synagogue at Capernaum .	7: 28–29	1: 21–28	4: 31–37
18. The healing of Peter's mother-in-law. Healings at evening .	8: 14–17	1: 29–34	4: 38–41
19. The withdrawal of Jesus. Preaching in Galilee	4: 23–25	1: 35–39	4: 42–44
20. The healing of a leper .	8: 1–4	1: 40–45	5: 12–16
(*c*) *Stories of conflict:*			
21. The healing of a paralytic . . .	9: 1–8	2: 1–12	5: 17–26
22. The call of Levi . .	9: 9–13	2: 13–17	5: 27–32
23. A question about fasting	9: 14–17	2: 18–22	5: 33–39
24. An incident in the cornfields on the Sabbath	12: 1–8	2: 23–28	6: 1–5
25. The healing of a man's withered hand .	12: 9–14	3: 1–6	6: 6–11
26. The retirement of Jesus. Acts of healing .	12: 15–21	3: 7–12	6: 17–19
27. The choosing of twelve disciples . . .	10: 1–4	3: 13–19	6: 12–16

	Matthew	Mark	Luke
28. The anxiety of Jesus' friends and the accusation of his enemies	12:22–37	3:20–30	11:14–23 12:10
29. Jesus' true family .	12:46–50	3:31–35	8:19–21

(*d*) *Parables of the Kingdom of God:*

	Matthew	Mark	Luke
30. The parable of the sower . . .	13: 1–9	4:1–9	8: 4–8
31. Jesus' use of parables .	13:10–15	4:10–12	8: 9–10
32. The meaning of the parable of the sower .	13:18–23	4:13–20	8:11–15
33. The parable of the lamp		4:21–25	8:16–18
34. The parable of the seed growing . . .		4:26–29	
35. The parable of the mustard seed . .	13:31–32	4:30–32	13:18–19
36. The method of parables	13:34–35	4:33–34	
37. The parable of the leaven . . .	13:33		13:20–21
38. The parable of the tares	13:24–30, 36–43		
39. The parables of the treasure and the pearl merchant . .	13:44–46		
40. The parable of the dragnet . . .	13:47–50		
41. The good householder .	13:51–52		
Note on parables			

(*e*) *The Great Sermon:*

	Matthew	Mark	Luke
Introductory note			
42. The beatitudes and the woes . . .	5: 1–12		6:17–26
43. The influence of salt and light . . .	5:13–16		14:34–35 11:33
44. Jesus and the Jewish Law	5:17–20		

	Matthew	*Mark*	*Luke*
45. On murder and reconciliation	5:21–26		12:57–59
46. On adultery and divorce	5:27–32		
47. On swearing	5:33–37		
48. On retaliation and loving one's enemies	5:38–48		6:27–36
49. Almsgiving	6: 1–4		
50. Prayer	6: 5–15		11: 1–4
51. Fasting	6:16–18		
52. The true treasure	6:19–21		12:33–34
53. The single eye	6:22–24		11:34–36 16:13
54. On anxiety	6:25–34		12:22–32
55. On judging others	7: 1–6		6:37–42
56. On asking	7: 7–11		11: 9–13
57. The Golden Rule	7:12		6:31
58. The narrow way	7:13–14		13:22–24
59. On fruit and the treasure of the heart	7:15–20		6:43–45
60. The confession of lordship. The parable of the two foundations	7:21–29		6:46–49 13:25–27
(*f*) *Further Galilaean activities*:			
61. The healing of the centurion's servant	8: 5–13		7: 1–10 13:28–30
62. The widow's son at Nain			7:11–17
63. The anointing in Simon's house			7:36–50
64. The women who ministered to Jesus			8: 1–3
65. The storm on the lake	8:23–27	4:35–41	8:22–25
66. The madman of the Gerasenes	8:28–34	5: 1–20	8:26–39
67. Jairus' daughter and the woman with haemorrhage	9:18–26	5:21–43	8:40–56

	Matthew	Mark	Luke
68. The healing of two blind men . .	9:27–31		
69. The healing of a dumb demoniac . .	9:32–34		
70. The rejection of Jesus at Nazareth . .	13:53–58	6: 1–6a	4:16–30
71. The mission of the twelve disciples .	10: 5–42	6:6b–13	9: 1–6
72. Herod's opinion of Jesus	14: 1–2	6:14–16	9: 7–9
73. The question of John from prison . .	11: 2–19		7:18–35
74. The death of John the Baptist . . .	14: 3–12	6:17–29	
75. The return of the twelve disciples. The feeding of the five thousand .	14:13–21	6:30–44	9:10–17
76. The journey across the lake . . .	14:22–36	6:45–56	
77. Jesus and scribal tradition . . .	15: 1–20	7: 1–23	

III. JOURNEYS IN THE NORTH

(*a*) *Phoenicia and other places outside Galilee:*

	Matthew	Mark	Luke
78. Tyre and Sidon: The Syro-Phoenician woman's daughter .	15:21–28	7:24–30	
79. Decapolis: the healing of a deaf stammerer .		7:31–37	
80. The feeding of the four thousand . .	15:29–39	8: 1–10	
81. The Pharisees' demand for a sign . .	16: 1–12	8:11–21	

(*b*) *Herod Philip's territory:*

	Matthew	Mark	Luke
82. The healing of a blind man at Bethsaida .		8:22–26	
83. Caesarea Philippi .	16:13–28	8:27–9:1	9:18–27
84. The transfiguration of Jesus . . .	17: 1–13	9: 2–13	9:28–36

	Matthew	Mark	Luke
85. The cure of an epileptic boy . . .	17:14–20	9:14–29	9:37–43a
(c) Return to Galilee:			
86. The second statement of the Passion . .	17:22–23	9:30–32	9:43b–45
87. Teaching on true greatness . . .	18: 1–5	9:33–37	9:46–48
88. The coin in the fish's mouth . . .	17:24–27		
89. A lesson on tolerance .		9:38–40	9:49–50
90. Teaching on offences and allied topics .	18: 6–14	9:41–50	17: 1–2
91. On the agreement of brethren. . .	18:15–20		
92. On forgiveness. The parable of the unmerciful servant . .	18:21–35		17: 3–4

IV. THE JOURNEY TO JERUSALEM

(a) The account in Mark:			
93. Judea: the question of divorce . . .	19: 1–12	10: 1–12	16:18
94. The reception of children . . .	19:13–15	10:13–16	18:15–17
95. The rich man . .	19:16–30	10:17–31	18:18–30
96. The parable of the labourers in the vineyard . . .	20: 1–16		
97. The third statement of the Passion . .	20:17–19	10:32–34	18:31–34
98. The request of James and John . .	20:20–28	10:35–45	
(b) Luke's travel-narrative:			
99. The beginning of the journey. The Samaritan village . .			9:51–56

	Matthew	Mark	Luke
120. The parable of the feast	22: 1–14		14:15–24
121. On taking up one's cross and counting the cost			14:25–35
122. Three parables of the lost . . .			15: 1–32
123. The parable of the dishonest steward .			16: 1–13
124. The self-righteousness of the Pharisees. The validity of the Jewish Law . . .			16:14–18
125. The parable of the rich man and Lazarus .			16:19–31
126. On faith and on service			17: 5–10
127. The healing of ten lepers			17:11–19
128. The coming of the kingdom and the day of the Son of Man .	24:26–28, 37–41		17:20–37
129. The parable of the unrighteous judge .			18: 1–8
130. The parable of the Pharisee and the tax-collector . .			18: 9–14
(c) Events at Jericho:			
131. The healing of blind Bartimaeus . .	20:29–34	10:46–52	18:35–43
132. The meeting with Zacchaeus . . .			19: 1–10
133. The parable of the pounds . . .			19:11–27
Note on miracles			

V. JESUS IN JERUSALEM

(a) Events of Holy Week

134. The entry into Jerusalem	21: 1–9	11: 1–11	19:28–44

	Matthew	Mark	Luke
152. The parable of the judgment . .	25:31–46		
(d) The Passion story:			
153. The conspiracy of the priests . . .	26: 1–5	14: 1–2	22: 1–2
154. The anointing at Bethany . . .	26: 6–13	14: 3–9	
155. The treachery of Judas	26: 14–16	14: 10–11	22: 3–6
156. The Last Supper .	26: 17–29	14: 12–25	22: 7–27
157. Warnings to the disciples and to Peter .	26: 30–35	14: 26–31	22: 28–39
158. Jesus in Gethsemane .	26: 36–56	14: 32–52	22: 40–53
159. Jesus before the High Priest . . .	26: 57–68	14: 53–65	22: 54–55, 63–71
160. The denials by Peter .	26: 69–75	14: 66–72	22: 56–62
161. The death of Judas .	27: 3–10		
162. Jesus before Pilate .	27: 1–2, 11–14	15: 1–5	23: 1–5
163. Jesus before Herod Antipas . .			23: 6–12
164. The condemnation of Jesus by Pilate .	27: 15–31	15: 6–20	23: 13–25
165. The crucifixion . .	27: 32–44	15: 21–32	23: 26–43
166. The death of Jesus .	27: 45–56	15: 33–41	23: 44–49
167. The burial of Jesus .	27: 57–66	15: 42–47	23: 50–56
(e) The resurrection			
168. The women's visit to the tomb	28: 1–15	16: 1–8	24: 1–12
169. The appearance in Galilee	28: 16–20		
170. A summary of resurrection appearances .		16: 9–20	
171. The walk to Emmaus .			24: 13–35
172. An appearance in Jerusalem . . .			24: 36–49
173. The ascension at Bethany			24: 50–53

I. JESUS' BIRTH AND BOYHOOD

(*a*) Matthew's Account

1. *The annunciation of the birth of Jesus*
Matthew 1 : 18–25

This story should be compared with that found in Luke (Section 5). They are from different sources, but have this in common, that Jesus' name was intimated before his birth, in the one case to Joseph and in the other to Mary.

Betrothal in Jewish law (19–20) was a binding act and could not be annulled without legal steps and payment. The betrothed man was technically the husband. The idea of God speaking to men through the appearance of *angels* (20) was widespread in Judaism after the Exile. Matthew is fond of giving instances of this. The name *Jesus* (Hebrew, *Jeshua*) bears a resemblance to the Hebrew for 'He shall save' (*joshea*).

The first introduction in Matthew of Old Testament prophecy is in 22–23. The word translated *virgin* meant in the Hebrew simply a young woman of marriageable age. The Old Testament passage (Isa. 7: 14) did not refer to the Messiah; it is about a 'sign' given to King Ahaz of Judah (about 735 B.C.), when he wanted proof of the presence and help of God. Isaiah told him that a baby would be born and given the name of Immanuel (meaning 'God is with us') as a sign of confidence by his parents. Before he should be able to differentiate between good and evil (i.e. come to manhood), the two enemies who threatened Judah, Syria and Israel, would be destroyed.

2. *The birth of Jesus. The visit of the Magi. The stay in Egypt. Settlement at Nazareth*

Matthew 2: 1–23

The *wise men* or Magi were Persians or Arabians, who would be Zoroastrians by religion and astrologers by profession. Later traditions said that they were kings and were three in number. The Old Testament passage in 5–6 is Micah 5: 2, which was probably regarded as Messianic by the early Christians. There were two ideas about the Messiah among the Jews—one that he would appear suddenly, no man knowing his origin, and the other that he would come from Bethlehem, which had been David's home town.

The *gifts* of the men (11) are products of Arabia. Gold was also found in Babylon, and frankincense (a sweet-smelling gum from a tree) in Persia and India. Myrrh was a resinous gum, used for ointment and embalming. The gifts are here intended to be symbolic.

King *Herod* here is Herod the Great, who died in 4 B.C. *Archelaus* (22) was his son (see p. 14). It is not stated how long the stay in Egypt lasted. The mention of *two years* (16) suggests that this was about the age of Jesus at the time of the Magi's visit.

The writer winds the story of the stay in Egypt around one Old Testament passage (15), the story of the Bethlehem massacre around another (18), and the residence at Nazareth around another (23). The quotation in 15 is from Hosea 11: 1, which is not a 'prophecy' but a statement of fact, about the Exodus of the Hebrews from Egypt. The quotation in 18 is from Jeremiah 31: 15. It referred to the departure of the exiles from Jerusalem after the fall of the city to the

Babylonians in 586 B.C., as they passed through Ramah. No Old Testament reference can be found for 23. Possibly the writer here confused Nazarene with Nazirite, thinking of Judges 13: 7, which was spoken of Samson. Another suggestion is that originally the quotation read, 'He shall be called Branch' (Hebrew, *nezer*)—the name of the Messianic king in Isaiah, Jeremiah and other Old Testament writers.

See the general note on the birth-stories, after Section 10.

(*b*) Luke's Account

3. *The prologue to Luke's Gospel*

Luke 1: 1–4

This paragraph is written in good literary Greek and is similar to the prologue usual at the beginning of a Greek book. Its dignity is well reproduced in the English versions.

Of the *many* referred to here (1), we know of two—the Gospel of Mark and the document Q. Luke suggests that there were others as well. He does not claim to be an eye-witness himself but to have received material from various sources. Nothing is known about *Theophilus*, to whom this book and Acts are dedicated. His title, *most excellent*, suggests that he was in a good social position and was possibly a Roman official.

4. *The annunciation of the birth of John the Baptist*

Luke 1: 5–25

Herod the king (5) is Herod the Great (see p. 14). *The course of Abijah* was one of twenty-four courses into which the service of the priesthood at Jerusalem was divided. Each was on duty twice a year, for a week at a time (1 Chron. 24: 10). It was decided by lot which priests should officiate and Zacharias' task was to *burn incense* before the altar (in the inner shrine) at the morning and evening sacrifices. The assistants withdrew before the incense was put on the coals, so Zacharias would be alone.

There is an Old Testament atmosphere about this story (8ff.). Other great men are said to have been announced before their births and the Old Testament prophets often declared that God had chosen them from birth. The name *John* (Hebrew, Johanan) means 'Yahweh is gracious', and was a common Jewish one (13). The abstinence from strong drink (15) reminds us of the vow of the Nazirites (Num. 6: 3); but nothing is said here about John's hair growing long, as was the Nazirite rule. The words in 17 are founded on Malachi 3: 1 and 4: 4–5, where it is said that Elijah would come before the Day of the Lord.

5. *The annunciation of the birth of Jesus*

Luke 1: 26–38

Compare the story in Matthew (Section 1) and see the general note on the birth-stories, after Section 10.

The hopes of the Jews in the first century about the Messiah are reflected in 32–33. These statements are not strictly correct about Jesus, for he did not have the earthly kingdom which is pictured here . . . Mary's answer to the angel (34) suggests a virgin birth, although it does not definitely state it. This is the only place in Luke where this tradition appears. There is some support in ancient authorities for reading here (instead of the answer of Mary in the English versions): 'Behold the hand-maid of the Lord . . .' (as in 38).

The relationship between Mary and Elizabeth is not stated (36). The popular idea is that they were sisters or cousins; in view of the differences between their ages, it is possible that Elizabeth was Mary's aunt.

6. *The meeting of Mary and Elizabeth*

Luke 1: 39–56

This scene links the story of the annunciation with that of the births of John and Jesus. The journey from Nazareth to *a city of Judea* (not named) would be seventy to eighty miles.

The Magnificat (46–56) is like an Old Testament psalm. There is the usual poetic structure, characterized by parallelism of phrases and ideas. The general theme is God's help to those who are faithful to him. There are also parallels with the Son of Hannah in 1 Samuel 2: 1–10. There is little in it which relates to Mary's case, apart from verse 48b. In some ancient manuscripts the name of Elizabeth occurs in verse 46 instead of Mary and it has been suggested that originally Luke simply wrote 'and she said'.

7. *The birth of John the Baptist*

Luke 1: 57–80

The story of Zacharias and Elizabeth is resumed from 1: 25 (Section 4). . . . Circumcision took place among the Jews on the eighth day after birth (59). Apparently the name of the child was also given on that occasion, although in Old Testament days this was given at birth. . . . Zacharias appears (from 62) to have been deaf as well as dumb.

The Benedictus (68ff.) is, like the Magnificat, a typical Jewish hymn—a Messianic psalm. The national privileges of the Jews are here enumerated. In 76–79 it deals with the immediate situation. Only in 76 is John spoken of as a forerunner, and there he is to *go before the face of the Lord.* 'The Lord' is a translation into Greek of the Old Testament name Yahweh, the God of the Hebrews. John is to be like an Old Testament prophet. Nothing is said about his being a forerunner of the Messiah or of his preaching about a greater one to come after him. . . . The *covenant* (72) is the usual Old Testament word for the bond between Israel and her God.

8. *The birth of Jesus. The visit of the shepherds*

Luke 2: 1–20

Both Luke and Matthew (see Sections 1–2) agree that Jesus was born before the death of Herod, which occurred in 4 B.C. Luke does not state this explicitly, but the phrase *in those days* (1) probably refers back to 1 : 5—*in the days of Herod the king.*

The date of the census (*enrolment*) under Quirinius (2) is not known. He was not actually governor until later, and a census took place then, in A.D. 6. That is probably why Luke refers to this as *the first enrolment.* Quirinius was a military commander in Syria in 8 B.C. There is evidence that periodical censuses were held in parts of the Roman Empire and that there was a fourteen-yearly cycle. This would give the date of the birth of Jesus as about 8 or 9 B.C. There is no evidence of a general world census such as Luke mentions here. His phrase *all the world* may mean simply 'the whole land' of Israel.

The reading of most manuscripts in 5 is *his betrothed wife.* Latin and Syriac manuscripts have simply 'his wife'. The betrothed woman, both among Jews and Romans, lived with her parents until her marriage. If Mary were only betrothed to Joseph, it seems strange that she should travel with him.

The story of *the shepherds* (8–20) suggests the springtime, when they would spend the night in the open country. . . . The Greek phrase in 14 is literally 'peace among men of [God's] good pleasure'. *Christ the Lord* (11) means 'The Lord Messiah' or 'An anointed Lord'.

9. *The presentation in the Temple. The return to Nazareth*

Luke 2: 21–40

Parents had to bring, according to Jewish law, an offering to the priests forty days after the birth of the first son (22), and the mother had to be purified (Lev. 12: 1–8).

The Nunc Dimittis (29–32) is a short poem reminiscent of Old Testament language. There is a wider outlook here, however. Jesus is intended not only for *the glory of thy people Israel* (the popular conception of the Messiah) but also for *a light for revelation to the Gentiles* (32). This phrase is from Isaiah 49: 6—one of the poems about the Servant of Yahweh.

A true description of the effect of Jesus' ministry is given in 34; some were attracted but many repelled. The *sword* to pass through Mary's heart is probably the sword of anguish or perhaps of doubt.

The phrase used about Anna (37) can mean that she had been a widow for eighty-four years, after seven years of married life. But it seems more natural to take it that she was a widow and was eighty-four years old. . . . Luke has a special interest in the Spirit of God (25–26) and in prophets (36).

10. *The boyhood of Jesus*

Luke 2: 41–52

This is the only story told in the New Testament about Jesus' boyhood. There are others, in later apocryphal Gospels, which are mainly flights of fancy, depicting Jesus as an infant prodigy and a wonder worker. In comparison with these, Luke's narrative is sober and restrained.

When a Jewish boy became twelve (42) he was—and still is—reckoned a 'son of the Law' and was considered grown-up. Jews of Palestine were expected to make three pilgrimages to Jerusalem each year—for the Passover, Pentecost and Tabernacles. But generally they made one. . . . The place where Jesus was found (46) would be the courts around the Temple building, where Jewish Rabbis (*the doctors*) used to sit and teach and discuss with their disciples. Jesus had joined one of these groups. Perhaps he was listening to a dispute between two groups of teachers and asking them questions about the points involved. Later traditions (and popular fancy) imagined him as putting questions to them and reducing them to silence. Luke simply says that he was *asking questions*—a very natural thing for a boy of twelve to do.

The Greek in 49 is literally 'in the things of my Father'. The rendering *in my Father's house* is the most probable and this is supported by evidence from contemporary writings where a similar phrase is used. . . . The fact that Joseph and Mary were worried about Jesus' behaviour and astonished at his actions and words suggests that this story was independent of the account of his birth, for they were evidently not prepared for this kind of thing on the part of Jesus.

General note on the birth stories

The accounts in Luke and Matthew differ in many respects. According to Luke 1: 26, Nazareth was the home of Joseph and Mary before the birth of Jesus and they went to Bethlehem only because of the Roman census. After the birth they returned *to their own city*, Nazareth (2: 39). In Matthew, however, it appears that Joseph and Mary lived in the neighbourhood of Jerusalem already. Later on they went to Nazareth, after a stay in Egypt of which Luke says nothing, in fulfilment of a 'prophecy' (Matthew 2: 23).

Matthew tells of the visit of the Magi and stresses the stir in Jerusalem, the interview with Herod, the search made for the child and the massacre of the children of Bethlehem. These events have left no trace in history and are difficult to reconcile with the obscurity associated with the beginning of Jesus' ministry. Luke tells of the Roman census, the visit of the worshipping shepherds and the prophecy of Simeon and Anna about the child.

It is difficult to account for the later attitude of Mary towards Jesus if she knew of the events narrated here. It is quite uncertain how far these stories are to be regarded as history and how far as poetic representations of the greatness of Jesus.

(*c*) Jesus' Family

11. *The genealogies*

Matthew 1: 1–17 Luke 3: 23–38

This is the family-tree of Jesus. Both genealogies give the ancestors of Joseph. The two lists agree only in the names from Abraham to David, where the Old Testament is followed.

Matthew in Jewish fashion places the genealogy at the beginning of the book. This list is artificially arranged in three groups of fourteen generations. This was a Rabbinic way of arranging such data, for use in committing to memory. The heading (1) means that Jesus was the Messiah (*the son of David*) and a true Jew (*the son of Abraham*). Luke traces the descent further back, to Adam and to God. His phrase in 23 (*as was supposed*) refers not to the fatherhood of Joseph but to the fact which Luke brings out at the close of the genealogy—that Jesus was really the son of the human race (Adam) and of God . . . Jesus' age (23—*about thirty*) is given somewhat roundly. If Jesus was born about 8 B.C., he would be older than this, for the work of John the Baptist (Section 12) is to be dated A.D. 28–29.

II. THE WORK OF JESUS IN GALILEE

(*a*) The Preaching of John the Baptist

12. *The message of John*

Matthew 3: 1–12 Mark 1: 1–8 Luke 3: 1–20

The opening verse in Mark is probably a heading to the whole book. The quotation from the Old Testament is a combination of Malachi 3: 1 and Isaiah 40: 3. The latter is from the work of the unknown prophet who wrote in the Exile in Babylon, referring to the hope of a return to Jerusalem. Mark says *in Isaiah.* Matthew corrected this by omitting the quotation from Malachi. . . . Matthew also adds that John preached about the Kingdom of God (or Heaven). This was the message of Jesus himself (Mark 1: 15; Matt. 4: 17) and it is generally thought that Matthew has here attributed Jesus' own message to John.

Luke prefaces his account with an elaborate date. Augustus Caesar died in A.D. 14, so *the fifteenth year of Tiberius* would be A.D. 28–29. But Tiberius had been associated with Augustus in the government of the provinces since A.D. 11; this date might therefore be A.D. 26. The former reckoning is the usual one today. *Pontius Pilate* was Roman procurator of Judea from A.D. 26–36. *Herod Antipas* was tetrarch of Galilee and Perea from 4 B.C. to A.D. 39. *Herod Philip* was tetrarch of Iturea and Trachonitis from 4 B.C. to A.D. 34. The only *Lysanias* known, until recently, as connected with Abilene was one who died in 36 or 34 B.C.; but an inscription has been found at Abila (the capital of

Abilene, near Damascus) referring to 'a freedman of Lysanias the tetrarch', dating from the time of Tiberius. So this confirms Luke here. *Annas* was deposed from the High Priesthood by the Romans in A.D. 15 and Caiaphas, his son-in-law, was High Priest from A.D. 18–38. . . . Luke's opening sounds like the formal beginning of a book and some think that the original draft of his Gospel began here.

The description of John's clothing in Mark and Matthew is taken partly from 2 Kings 1:8—a description of Elijah. His diet of *locusts* may have been the insect, which can be cooked and eaten, or the locust-bean, the pods of the carob tree. The word *baptize* means literally 'dip'. Ritual washing for the removal of defilement was common among the Jews, and Jewish proselytes were baptized. What was remarkable about John was his authority to remit sins by baptism and the fact that he baptized Jews.

The message of John. Both Matthew (7–10) and Luke (7–9) add to Mark some matter from Q. John used vivid metaphors in denouncing his hearers. The *vipers* are pictured as fleeing from the field when the harvest begins. The picture may, however, be that of a fire, frequent in the thick scrub in the Jordan valley, from which the snakes seek to escape. *The wrath to come* is a reference to the coming 'Day of the Lord', when the judgment on sinners would be carried out. The Jews considered this as destined for the heathen only. John said that even the *sons of Abraham* (the Jews themselves) would be called to account. There is probably a play upon words here. *Stones*, in the Aramaic in which John spoke, is *abānim*, while *children* is *bānim*.

John and the coming one. John stated that he was the forerunner of *one mightier than I*, but he did not specify this as the Messiah. Again he used vivid pictorial language. *Fire* stands for destruction and also cleansing. To *undo* or *carry sandals* was the work of a slave. The *fan* was a wooden winnowing shovel, from which the farmer threw the grain against the wind to separate it from the chaff, which then fell to the ground and was gathered up and burnt.

John's ethical teaching. Luke adds particulars of John's advice to different people (10–14). The *coat* (11) was the undergarment, as opposed to the outer cloak. The two might be worn in travelling, but both were not essential. (cf. Luke 6: 29; Matt. 5: 40). The *publicans* (12) in the Gospels are subordinate tax-collectors. They were held in low esteem by both Jews and Gentiles. The *soldiers* (14) may have been Romans, but were more probably Jews—possibly soldiers of Herod. . . . Luke adds a note about the imprisonment of John (19–20). This is reported later in Mark (6: 17 ff.—see Section 74).

13. *The baptism of Jesus by John*

Matthew 3: 13–17   Mark 1: 9–11   Luke 3: 21–22

The account here employs Eastern symbolism. Mark says the Spirit came to Jesus *as a dove.* This does not mean the presence of an actual dove but describes the influence of the Spirit on Jesus. Some Old Testament prophets and writers had tended to think of the Spirit of God as a violent and extraordinary influence; here it comes in a peaceful and gentle manner. Luke alone has *in bodily form.* He does tend to 'materialize' the expressions he finds in his sources.

The *voice* indicates the call of God and Jesus' response. The words are a combination of quotations from

Psalms 2: 7 and Isaiah 42: 1. The first passage is addressed to a Jewish king and was regarded as Messianic, while the second relates to the 'servant' of God portrayed in the latter part of 'Isaiah'. So this narrative means that Jesus realized here that he was to be the Messiah and God's Servant.

Matthew adds words of protest by John at Jesus' coming to him for baptism, and Jesus' answer (14–15). This is probably a later explanation why Jesus submitted to baptism. This process was carried a stage further later on, and apocryphal Gospels recorded conversations between Jesus and John. The real reason for Jesus' action was probably that he wished to associate himself with the expectations of the people who followed John.

14. *The temptations of Jesus*

Matthew 4: 1–11 Mark 1: 12–13 Luke 4: 1–13

Mark gives a brief statement, while Matthew and Luke take their account from Q. The *forty days* in the wilderness indicate a round number. The place was the desert region on the west of the Dead Sea. At his baptism Jesus had received his call. The question now presented itself: What sort of a Messiah was he to be? There were current popular ideas and expectations of the Messiah. Some hoped for a political leader, who would restore the nation to its former greatness and set up an earthly kingdom. Others expected a figure to appear in a marvellous way; some spoke of a supernatural 'Son of Man' to come on the clouds and astonish men by the 'signs' which he did. Others had a more spiritual notion.

This story is a symbolic account of Jesus' struggle as

he faced the choices before him. He rejected three ways of going about his work:

(i) Bribery, to *turn stones into bread.* Jesus was probably thinking of the hungry people of Palestine, not his own state of hunger. He was tempted to feed them physically, instead of concentrating on his spiritual message (the *word of God*). The real temptation probably lies in the *if*—the suggestion to doubt his own experience at his baptism.

(ii) Magic—the temptation to do something wonderful, as was expected of the Messiah. The *pinnacle of the Temple* is literally the 'little wing' of the Temple buildings at Jerusalem. To descend from there would be to attract crowds. Jesus saw that such action would not be 'trusting' God but tempting him, i.e. putting him to the test. This temptation is put second in Matthew but third in Luke.

(iii) The way of force and worldly might. Jesus could gain all *the kingdoms of the world* if he took the way of the world conquerors. He realized that this would be serving evil instead of worshipping God.

Jesus gains support for his stand by reference to his Bible—the Old Testament—in each case (see Deut. 8: 3, 6: 16, 6: 13 and 10: 21).

(*b*) Jesus' Preaching and Healing

15. *Jesus' return to Galilee. The call of four disciples*
Matthew 4: 12–22 Mark 1: 14–20 Luke 4: 14–15

The imprisonment of John the Baptist seems to have been the reason for Jesus' return to Galilee and the beginning of his public preaching. Matthew typically adds to the account in Mark a quotation from the Old Testament—Isaiah 9: 1–2.

Mark (14–15) well summarizes Jesus' message. *Gospel* means 'good news'. *The Kingdom of God* meant the Reign of God rather than an external Kingdom. It is possible that the phrase here should be translated: 'The Kingdom of God has arrived.'

Jesus was probably already acquainted with the four fishermen whom he called to be disciples. They may have been disciples of John the Baptist. Luke omits this passage; he has another story about the call of Peter (next section).

16. *The call of Peter and the catch of fish*

Luke 5: 1–11

Luke places this after Jesus' preaching in Capernaum and Nazareth, but it is put here for comparison with the previous section. James and John are here spoken of as partners with Simon, but nothing is said about Andrew.

The Lake of Gennesaret (1) is the Lake of Galilee. Gennesaret was a plain south of Capernaum. Peter had apparently been fishing in the shallow waters near the shore; Jesus told him to *put out into the deep* (4). There is no suggestion here that Jesus suddenly created the fish or made the shoal arrive at the spot where the boat was. If there is any 'miracle' in this story, it would be in Jesus' perception of the place where the fish could be caught.

There is a somewhat similar story in John 21: 1–14 (see Section V in Part II).

17. *Jesus in the synagogue at Capernaum*

Matthew 7: 28–29 <u>Mark 1: 21–28</u> Luke 4: 31–37

Capernaum is probably the modern Tell Hum, on the north-west coast of the Lake of Galilee. In Mark this is Jesus' first preaching in a synagogue. Matthew omits the incident, but uses a phrase from Mark to conclude the Sermon on the Mount (Matt. 5–7).

In the synagogue service it was permitted for any male adult to read the lesson and to preach, on the invitation of the ruler of the synagogue. The invitation was often extended to distinguished visitors. The reaction of the people at Jesus' teaching, their astonishment that he spoke *with authority, and not as the scribes*, suggests that the latter used to teach by referring to traditional authorities. The pupils of the Rabbis taught what was delivered to them; Jesus' teaching was original.

Mark describes a typical case of exorcism, i.e. the driving out of evil spirits. Everybody in the first century believed the world was filled with demons under the leadership of a prince of evil. Disease, particularly mental disorder, was attributed to demon-possession. We should probably say the man was afflicted with a form of hysteria. With his insight, however, he was able to recognize Jesus and his mission as *the Holy One of God.* Jesus' rebuke, *Hold thy peace*, is literally 'be muzzled'. It was a term used to express the binding of persons possessed with evil spirits.

18. *The healing of Peter's mother-in-law. Healings at evening*

Matthew 8: 14–17 <u>Mark 1: 29–34</u> Luke 4: 38–41

Matthew and Luke both abbreviate Mark. The phrase about Peter's mother-in-law—*she lay sick of a fever*—is altered by Luke to *stricken with a great fever*. This was a phrase used by doctors and may indicate malaria. The fact that Peter (and other apostles) were married is confirmed by Paul (1 Cor. 9: 5).

There follows a generalized account of a typical scene of healing. The end of the Sabbath came at sunset. Matthew and Luke have each left out part of Mark's redundant phrase, *when evening came, when the sun set.* Mark says the people brought *all* sick and possessed and Jesus healed *many.* Matthew alters this to state that they brought *many* and Jesus healed *all* of them, thus avoiding the implication that some were not healed

19. *The withdrawal of Jesus. Preaching in Galilee*
Matthew 4: 23–25 Mark 1: 35–39 Luke 4: 42–44

The *desert place* would be simply a lonely spot outside the city. Some think that Jesus deliberately left Capernaum because he was in danger of being regarded and followed as a healer and wonder-worker, rather than as a teacher. . . . The phrase in Mark *for to this end came I forth* (38) may mean simply: 'That is why I left Capernaum.' Luke interprets it to refer to Jesus' mission: *therefore was I sent* (43). There follows a general statement of Jesus' preaching work in Galilee.

20. *The healing of a leper*
Matthew 8: 1–4 Mark 1: 40–45 Luke 5: 12–16

Matthew and Luke both follow Mark, but the situation is different. In Mark it is after Jesus' departure from Capernaum, when preaching in Galilee. In Matthew it is after he had come from the hillside, after giving the Sermon on the Mount (Matt. 5–7). In Luke it is after the call of Peter (Section 16).

Lepers were forbidden to come into contact with other people or to enter houses. They had to give warning of their approach by a cry. *Leprosy*, however, was used of a number of skin diseases in the first century.

By touching the leper, Jesus made himself 'unclean', according to the Law. Mark uses strong expressions about Jesus' emotion and action. The phrase *being moved with compassion* (41) should probably be 'being angry', while *sent him out* (43) is literally 'thrust him out'. Perhaps Jesus was angry at the suggestion in the man's words, *If thou wilt* . . . implying that the man doubted Jesus' willingness to heal him; or the anger of Jesus may have been directed against the conditions of the time which allowed such things to be.

Jesus' command to the man was twofold. (i) Not to say anything to anybody—a common feature in Mark after a miracle of healing. Jesus did not want to be harassed by crowds who would come to be healed or to see other people cured. (ii) To obey the Jewish Law, which stated that if a man considered himself cured of leprosy he had to be certified clean by a priest and then had to offer sacrifices for his purification (Lev. 14: 1ff). Here Jesus enjoined observance of the Law, as it was obviously of advantage to all concerned. The words *as a testimony to them* may mean as a public witness to the people in general, or as an assurance to the priests that Jesus kept the Law.

(*c*) Stories of Conflict

21. *The healing of a paralytic*

Matthew 9: 1–8 Mark 2: 1–12 Luke 5: 17–26

This is the first of a series of incidents (Mark 2: 1–3: 6—Sections 21–25) in which Jesus comes into conflict with the Jewish religious leaders. Here the reason is that Jesus showed his authority in two ways—by declaring to the man that his sins had been forgiven and by commanding him to walk.

The phrase *sick of the palsy* is literally 'a paralytic'. The man was obviously paralysed in his legs. . . . Mark thinks of a Palestinian house with a roof of dried mud, which the man's four friends *broke up* (4). Luke thinks rather of a Roman roof with tiles, through which they *let him down* (19). . . . There was apparently in this man's case a connection between his previous sinful life and his physical condition. To the scribes who complained of Jesus' words to the man the vindication of Jesus' claim that his sins were forgiven would be the restoration of his physical health.

The term *Son of Man* is used here for the first time in the Gospels. It had a long history. In the book of Daniel the author describes a vision of wild animals or beasts (representing the world empires), and then there comes *one like the son of man* (Dan. 7: 13–14). This is a Hebrew phrase for a human being, and the writer explains later that he means 'the kingdom of the saints of the Most High', i.e. the nation of Israel. In two later Jewish books written about 100 B.C., the Son of Man becomes a definite person—a supernatural Messiah who would come in glory on the clouds. In some places in the Gospels this thought seems to be reflected in Jesus' use of the term. Here, however this idea seems out of place, and it has been suggested that the phrase means simply 'man'. Jesus says that man on earth has authority to pronounce the forgiveness of sins granted by God. This claim would scandalize the Jews, who held that only God could do this. The comment of the crowd in Matthew (8) seems to support this interpretation. Others, however, consider that Jesus here meant himself. A third suggestion is that 10 of Mark should be omitted, as a parenthesis, being originally the remark of a Christian preacher telling the story. The account certainly runs more smoothly without it.

22. *The call of Levi*

Matthew 9: 9–13 Mark 2: 13–17 Luke 5: 27–32

Levi would probably be a collector of taxes in the service of Herod Antipas—perhaps an excise man on the Damascus road through Capernaum. 'Matthew' calls him Matthew and so identifies him with the apostle. Mark and Luke do not actually say that he became one of the intimate circle, although his call reads like that.

The call of the despised tax-collector is linked with another complaint of the religious authorities against Jesus—that he ate with disreputable people. The scribes and Pharisees were shocked that one who professed to be a religious teacher should associate with *publicans and sinners*—people who did not strictly keep to the Jewish Law. . . . Jesus' reply, *They that are whole have no need of a physician*, may be a quotation from a popular proverb. *To call the sinners* may mean: to invite them to my company. Luke adds *to repentance*, and so obscures the point. Jesus was using the term *righteous* ironically here, alluding to those who thought themselves righteous or pure in God's sight.

23. *A question about fasting*

Matthew 9: 14–17 Mark 2: 18–22 Luke 5: 33–39

This is another conflict-story. Matthew changes Mark so that John the Baptist's disciples make the complaint. Jesus and his disciples were apparently ignoring some Jewish ritual fast. It has been suggested that the incident took place after the death of John and his disciples were fasting in mourning for him. But it is unlikely if the Pharisees would join in this.

The *sons of the bridechamber* mentioned in Jesus' reply are the companions of the bridegroom—the groomsmen. The wedding festivities among the Jews were continued for seven days among the bridegroom's friends, while he was with them. In Matthew 11: 16–19 and Luke 7: 31–35 (Section 73) Jesus again suggests a comparison between his company and a wedding party. . . . There follows the first indication of Jesus' foreboding of his own fate—the bridegroom *will be taken away*. Some think the words are unsuitable here and are a later Christian addition to the story.

The parabolic saying about the patch (the meaning of *that which should fill it up*) and the wine are remarks about the difficulty of combining old and new. The traditional religion of Judaism could not be patched up to make Jesus' teaching fit it; it was impossible to contain his new wine in the old receptacles. The *wine skins* were of leather; in them new wine ferments and they should 'give'. But old skins would not, and so would burst when the new wine was put into them.

24. *An incident in the cornfields on the Sabbath*

Matthew 12: 1–8 Mark 2: 23–28 Luke 6: 1–5

This is the first of the controversies in the Gospels about the Sabbath. Plucking the ears of corn or rubbing them with the hands was counted by the Rabbis to be equivalent to reaping and threshing, and so was considered work, which was forbidden on the Sabbath. The time indicated here is the spring.

Jesus' reply is three-fold. He first pointed out that even the Law must be subservient to human needs. He gave a case from Hebrew history, about David. It is not a perfect parallel, because the incident did not happen on the Sabbath, but is a general statement of the principle. The name of the High Priest was not Abiathar, as Mark says, but Ahimelech (1 Sam. 21: 1ff). Matthew and Luke both omit the name. The *shewbread* was twelve loaves of wheaten bread, placed in the Holy Place each Sabbath, which were eaten by the priests at the end of the week.

Jesus then enunciates two principles (27–28 in Mark). about the use and value of the Sabbath. The addition in Matthew (5–7) seems to break the connection and was probably added from another source or occasion. . . . The term *Son of Man* in the final statement (cf. Mark 2: 10) has been taken to mean: (i) Jesus himself; (ii) his disciples, as representatives of the Messianic community; (iii) man in general, since the Sabbath was made for him. Some think this sentence is a later comment by a Christian preacher.

In one Greek manuscript of Luke, the following is added at the close of this narrative: 'On the same day, beholding someone working on the Sabbath, he said to him: "Man, if thou knowest what thou art doing, thou art blessed; but if thou knowest not, thou art accursed and a transgressor of the Law."' This may be a genuine saying of Jesus, the purpose of which was to make people think out for themselves the purpose of the Sabbath law.

25. *The healing of a man's withered hand*

Matthew 12: 9–14 Mark 3: 1–6 Luke 6: 6–11

This is the conclusion of this series of stories and the last verse is the climax—a plot to destroy Jesus.

The Pharisees considered it lawful to heal on the Sabbath only when life was in danger. Here they may have deliberately introduced the man into Jesus' presence as a trap. The point of Jesus' reply is that for Semites healing was equivalent to 'making alive'—*to save a life*. Hence to leave the man alone would be equivalent to killing him. Some have thought that Jesus was making a covert reference to the intention of his enemies to have *him* put to death. Matthew adds a saying (11–12) which is paralleled in Luke 14: 5 (Section 118).

The Herodians (in 6 of Mark) are found elsewhere only in Mark 12: 13 (Matt. 22: 16), where they are again allied with the Pharisees. They were probably politically minded people who were partisans of the Herod family.

A lost Gospel, the *Gospel according to the Nazarenes*, is said to have contained this statement, made by the man to Jesus: 'I am a mason, seeking my living by my hands. I pray thee, Jesus, that thou wouldst restore my health, that I may not shamefully beg my food.'

26. *The retirement of Jesus. Acts of healing*

Matthew 12: 15–21 Mark 3: 7–12 Luke 6: 17–19

Mark describes a number of typical scenes in the ministry of Jesus. Matthew adds a quotation from the

Servant Poems (Isa. 42: 1ff), while in Luke the passage is an introduction to the 'Sermon on the Plain'.

Idumaea (in 8 of Mark) is the Edom of the Old Testament. It had been conquered by the Jews about 128 B.C. and was now considered Jewish territory. The district *beyond Jordan* was Perea, the land between the rivers Jabbok and Arnon, east of the Jordan and the Dead Sea.

Mark suggests in other places also (11) that the demons and spirits recognized Jesus before men did, but that Jesus did not allow them to make his secret public (cf. Mark 1: 24–25).

27. *The choosing of twelve disciples*

Matthew 10: 1–4 | Mark 3: 13–19 | Luke 6: 12–16

The names of the twelve apostles are given here and in Acts 1: 13. The word *apostle* means 'one sent out'. It was used originally of an ambassador and then generally for an envoy or messenger.

Some of the disciples had special names or titles. Simon was called Peter, meaning a rock. It did not describe his character but was a promise and an encouragement. Boanerges, or *sons of thunder*, means the 'stormy, thunderous ones'. Simon the Cananaean (Mark and Matt.) or the Zealot (Luke) may have been a member of the fanatical nationalistic party (see p. 13). *Cananaean* does not mean from Canaan or Cana but is a transliteration of a Hebrew word meaning zealous. *Iscariot*, the name of Judas, may mean a man of Kerioth, which was a place in the south. If so, Judas was not a Galilaean like the others. But the real meaning of the title is uncertain.

28. *The anxiety of Jesus' friends and the accusation of his enemies*

Matthew 12: 22–37 Mark 3: 20–30 Luke 11: 14–23
12: 10

The short statement about the anxiety of Jesus' friends is found only in Mark (20–21). Perhaps the other two writers omitted it from motives of reverence. The phrase translated *his friends* is literally 'those about him', i.e. his acquaintances and possibly the members of his family. This incident may therefore be connected with that in Section 29. The statement *They said, He is beside himself* may mean 'People were saying, He is mad' or it may be the verdict of his own family.

The story about the accusation of Jesus' enemies was included both in Mark and in Q, for Luke and Matthew seem to be following the latter document here. *Beelzebub* should be Beelzebul. There is some doubt as to the real meaning of the term. It was the name of a Philistine god in Old Testament times (2 Kings 1: 2ff.). The original may have meant 'lord of the lofty house', i.e. lord of heaven, like the Greek Zeus. Then the word was spelt Beelzebub, meaning 'lord of flies'—a term of contempt. A slight variation would make this 'lord of refuse'. But the Aramaic word for 'flies' is somewhat similar to that for 'enmity', so Beelzebub may have been used as another rendering of 'the enemy', i.e. the devil.

Jesus' enemies did not deny his power but attributed it to another cause than the true one. Jesus' reply (in 24–29 of Mark) is three-fold. In the middle of it Matthew and Luke insert another argument, from the passage in Q, where Jesus points out the true origin of his power—that he uses the authority of God, and therefore the Kingdom of God has arrived.

Blasphemy against the Holy Spirit seems to mean the tendency to ascribe to an evil power that which is obviously due to the work of the Spirit of God. It is the failure to differentiate between good and evil; this renders a man incapable of moral discrimination. Such a man *hath never forgiveness, but is guilty of an eternal sin. Eternal* here does not mean everlasting. It is the quality of the sin which is stressed—sin in its fullness as eternal life is life in its fullness.

29. *Jesus' true family*

Matthew 12: 46–50 Mark 3: 31–35 Luke 8: 19–21

Mark's story is often taken as the sequel of the anxiety of Jesus' friends (3: 20–21). There are three views about Jesus' *brethren*, mentioned here and elsewhere in the New Testament (cf. Mark 6: 3). (i) That they were the children of Joseph by a former wife, before he married Mary. No trace of such a wife can, however, be found. (ii) That they were Jesus' cousins (the view of Jerome). (iii) That they were his brothers, the children of Mary born after Jesus. The Greek of the Gospels (and the other New Testament references) uses the ordinary Greek word for 'brothers' and 'sisters' when speaking of the other members of Jesus' family.

In his reply Jesus does not repudiate the family relationship, but points out that his true family is wider than this. As elsewhere in his teaching, there is an insistence here on *doing* the will of God.

(*d*) Parables of the Kingdom of God

30. *The parable of the sower*

Matthew 13: 1–9 Mark 4: 1–9 Luke 8: 4–8

In Mark (chapter 4) there is a collection of parables about the Kingdom of God. Matthew reproduced these (chapter 13) and added other parables, from other sources, thus making one of the great discourses of Jesus in this Gospel. See the note on parables, after Section 41.

This is an introductory parable, more about preaching than about the Kingdom of God. The sower was of course sowing 'broadcast', throwing the seed to right and left as he walked down the path. The reception given to the seed in different types of soil is described. *The way side* would be the path running across the field. *The rocky ground* would be the rock beneath the soil where it would be thin. *The thorns* are the roots which have been left still in the soil. They creep up after the sowing and choke the wheat when it begins to grow.

31. *Jesus' use of parables*

Matthew 13: 10–15 Mark 4: 10–12 Luke 8: 9–10

The statement made by Jesus and the Old Testament quotation (Isa. 6: 9–10) seem to suggest two classes of people—the disciples and 'those outside'. The former understand *the mystery of the Kingdom* but parables are told in order that the latter shall not see, hear and understand, as if the purpose of Jesus' parables was to obscure his meaning instead of illuminating it. This difficulty was seen by Matthew, who altered the phrasing of Mark.

This, however, seems plainly counter to Jesus' teaching and his intention, which was to illuminate the truth, not to hide it. Two considerations help here. (i) To the Hebrew mind this would not seem so purposive as it does to us. The quotation from Isaiah 6 may describe the *result* of the teaching by parables, not the *purpose* for which Jesus used them. Isaiah realized at the beginning of his public work that the result of his preaching among people stubborn and unwilling to accept him would be that they would become hardened and deaf and blind. Jesus may have felt that in this respect his work was to be like Isaiah's. (ii) It is possible that the first word in 12 of Mark translates an Aramaic word which meant 'who'. The quotation then describes the people who *are without*—they are the people who *see but do not perceive*, etc. (See T.W. Manson, *The Teaching of Jesus*.)

Some think that the quotation from Isaiah 6 was not actually given by Jesus on this occasion, but was added by Mark to the words in 11. Mark, or some early Christian preacher, may have felt the reception of Jesus' words was a fulfilment of prophecy and so provided here a suitable quotation.

The mystery of the kingdom. This is the only time that the word *mystery* occurs in the Gospels. In the New Testament it is frequent in Paul's letters and means a secret now revealed. The meaning here may be: (i) that Christianity is a mystery religion, like the mystery-cults in the Hellenistic world, into which people could be initiated; (ii) that the secret revealed to Jesus' disciples was the method he was to use to establish the Kingdom; (iii) that the secret was the fact that the Kingdom had arrived, in the ministry of Jesus himself.

32. *The meaning of the parable of the sower*

Matthew 13: 18–23   Mark 4: 13–20   Luke 8: 11–15

The parable of the sower does not seem to need much 'explanation' and there are two difficulties among the interpretations given here. (i) The interpretation makes the parable into an allegory—a story in which each detail stands for something else, in another realm. This is unlike the method of Jesus' teaching. (ii) The explanation does not fit the parable. In the parable different results are produced because of the different kinds of soil on which the seed falls, but in this explanation there are different kinds of seed, which symbolize different types of people. In the parable the emphasis is on the good results which come in spite of disappointments. In the explanation the emphasis is on the seeds which fail to produce fruit.

The conclusion generally held today is that this represents not the teaching of Jesus but the comments of a Christian teacher, the interpretation given to the parable in Mark's day. The parable itself is simpler than this elaborate attempt to explain it.

33. *The parable of the lamp*

Mark 4: 21–25   Luke 8: 16–18

There are parallels to many of these sayings in other parts of the Gospels. See Matthew 13: 12, 5: 13 (Luke 11: 33), 10: 26 (Luke 12 : 2), 7: 2 (Luke 6: 38), 25: 29 (Luke 19: 26).

The *bushel* in Mark (21) is a peck measure. Verse 22 is an example of the poetic form of much of Jesus' teaching, with its parallelism of synonymous clauses. . . . The meaning of these sayings seems to be: The function of a lamp is not to be hidden but to shed light. So the truth that Jesus had to proclaim, although for the time being it seemed to be hidden from the crowds, would ultimately be revealed. The meaning in 24 of Mark is: Take care what you listen to and do not judge people harshly. Luke changes this to mean: Be careful how you hear, for he who hears rightly will be capable of receiving yet more truths.

34. *The parable of the seed growing*
Mark 4: 26–29

This is the only parable of Jesus which is found only in Mark. The Kingdom is here thought of as growing without our continually worrying about its progress, just as *the earth beareth fruit of herself*. The growth may be secret and slow at first but all the time it is steady and it is ultimately due to God.

Some have thought that this is Jesus' answer to an attempt to link him with the Zealot movement, to hasten the coming of God's Kingdom. C. H. Dodd (see *The Parables of the Kingdom*) says that the point of the parable is in the last verse, where Jesus proclaims that the time of harvest has now come; the Kingdom is again stated by Jesus to have arrived.

35. *The parable of the mustard seed*
Matthew 13: 31–32 Mark 4: 30–32 Luke 13: 18–19

This parable occurred in both Mark and Q. Luke follows the latter version, while Matthew conflates Mark and Q.

There appears to have been a Jewish proverb: 'Small as a grain of mustard seed'. In Palestine mustard plants sometimes grow to a height of six feet. The point of the parable is in the great contrast between the small seed and the big plant. . . . A tree was a recognized metaphor for a great empire. *The birds of the heaven* may represent the nations of the world—another indication that Jesus thought of more than a national Jewish Kingdom. Dodd sees here the same emphasis as in the previous parable—the plant has grown, the Kingdom has come and already men are flowing into it.

36. *The method of parables*
Matthew 13: 34–35 Mark 4: 33–34

This is a summary, to conclude Mark's collection of parables of the Kingdom. Matthew adds a quotation from the Old Testament (Ps. 78: 2)—not strictly *by the prophet*.

37. *The parable of the leaven*
Matthew 13: 33 Luke 13: 20–21

Leaven (yeast) has generally a bad name in the Bible, standing for evil influence. Here, however, it represents the hidden—but revolutionary—power of the Kingdom. The point of the parable may again be in the end of it—the leaven is now at work, in the ministry of Jesus. . . . Possibly there is a reminiscence of Jesus' home life here, when he watched his mother making bread, being careful to mix the yeast with the meal.

38. *The parable of the tares*
Matthew 13: 24–30, 36–43

The *tares* (or darnel) grow as high as the wheat, but are not generally pulled up until harvest. Jesus was thus recounting a procedure familiar to farmers. He may have been enforcing his own precept—'Judge not', i.e. do not attempt to condemn now; the harvest of the Kingdom will show up the tares.

The parable is frequently applied to the Christian Church, in which are to be found worthy and unworthy members. But in the New Testament the Church is never equated with the Kingdom. Jesus' original meaning was more probably that in the world the people are mixed, but when the Kingdom comes they are sorted out. He may have wished to stress the presence of the Kingdom there and then; men were already being sorted out, by his presence among them. The setting here, however, is eschatological, i.e. the coming of the Kingdom is pictured as among the 'last things' (30).

In the interpretation (36–43) this is brought out clearly. This explanation labours under the same difficulty as that for the parable of the sower (Section 32)—that it makes the parable into an elaborate allegory where every item means precisely something in the affairs of men. This is probably a later explanation of the parable, which was current in the Church when Matthew was written.

Sons of the Kingdom (38) means those whose characters fit them for the Kingdom. *Sons of the evil* [*one*] means those whose characters are evil. The *harvest* as a metaphor for the end, the Day of the Lord, is found frequently in the Old Testament. The *Son of Man* is introduced here as the conventional apocalyptic figure, bringing judgment to the world.

39. *The parables of the treasure and the pearl merchant*
Matthew 13: 44–46

These two 'twin' parables illustrate the eagerness which is necessary in order to find the Kingdom. The two men are of different types—one a poor farm labourer and the other an experienced jeweller—but they are both keen and willing to make sacrifices in order to obtain treasure. Another point of difference between the two parables is that in the first the man came upon the treasure unexpectedly, whereas in the second the merchant was engaged in his ordinary business of seeking for pearls when he found the one of great price. So Jesus suggests that people come to the Kingdom in different ways and discover its value. . . . Perhaps the previous owner of the field (44) had gone on a foreign journey and had never returned. It was a common practice to hide treasure in the earth (cf. Matt. 25: 25), especially if one did not trust the bankers of those days.

40. *The parable of the dragnet*
Matthew 13: 47–50

This is similar to the parable of the tares (Section 38). It points out that not all who hear the message of the Kingdom are worthy and the coming of the Kingdom means the selection and judgment of men. The last two verses are like the conclusion of the parable of the tares and may represent the interpretation of the Church.

The *net* is a large dragnet, as distinct from the smaller nets which the fishers were using when Jesus called them from the lakeside.

41. *The good householder*
Matthew 13: 51–52

This is the conclusion of the parables in Matthew 13. It seems to commend the disciples, because they have understood the parables. . . . This saying somewhat counter-balances Jesus' judgment elsewhere on the Jewish scribes. If scribes became his followers they would be especially valuable, as they could use their old training and knowledge, in addition to the new light they received. It has been remarked that this well describes the author of Matthew. He was *a scribe instructed in the Kingdom of Heaven.*

Note on parables

The word *parable* is derived from two Greek words—*para* (by the side of) and *ballo* (I put). A parable is thus a comparison between two things which are put together for this purpose. Parables are neither allegories nor fables. The former are elaborate stories in which each item or person represents something or somebody. Fables are imaginary tales, to point a moral.

Jesus' parables are of two types. (i) True comparisons, in which something in the world of men or of nature is compared with the Kingdom of God or the character of God himself. Most of the parables in the preceding sections are of this type. (ii) Illustrative stories, to portray some praiseworthy feat of human conduct or thought. These are found almost exclusively in Luke, e.g., the Good Samaritan, the Prodigal Son, the Pharisee and the tax-collector. In these parables men are held up as examples to follow. There is no strict comparison and these are not to be classed among the parables of the Kingdom.

Matthew generally uses the phrase *Kingdom of Heaven* whereas Mark uses *Kingdom of God.* The two terms mean the same. The Jews often wished to avoid using the term God, out of reverence, and substituted titles such as 'the Power', 'the King' or 'Heaven'. The writer of Matthew has here substituted Heaven for God.

(*e*) The Great Sermon

Introductory note

Sections 42–60 consist of matter which is found in the Sermon on the Mount (Matt. 5–7). Luke, however, has a discourse of Jesus, often called the Sermon on the Plain (Luke 6: 17–49), delivered on *a level place*, while that in Matthew was delivered on *the mountain.* There is a close resemblance in structure and in contents between the two. They have the same beginning (beatitudes) and the same ending (the parable of the two foundations) and both are closely followed by the story of the healing of a centurion's servant. Nearly all the Lukan matter is found in Matthew 5–7. The order of Jesus' teaching in the two accounts is practically the same. The Sermon in Matthew, however, is much longer and contains additional material. Some of this is found in other places in Luke, but much of it has no parallel elsewhere.

Did Jesus give one such address or two? The probable solution is that the matter in the two Sermons which is parallel was taken by both writers from the document Q. Luke may preserve more nearly the order of the matter in Q; the writer of Matthew then added matter from other places in Q and also teaching from his own special source or traditions. He arranged it in the form of an elaborate discourse. Two themes are dealt with in particular, in Matthew: the moral character of Jesus' followers and the relation between his new teaching and the Jewish laws and customs. Both accounts are thus really compilations of Jesus' teaching, delivered probably on several separate occasions.

The reason why Matthew pictures Jesus as on a mountain delivering this discourse may be that the first Law was given to Moses on Mount Sinai and he feels this a fitting parallel. Another possible explanation is that he was thinking of Isaiah 40: 9—Jesus goes to a mountain to deliver the 'good news'.

42. *The beatitudes and the woes*
Matthew 5: 1–12 Luke 6: 17–26

The beatitudes constitute Jesus' estimate of the people who are really *blessed* or *happy* (as the Greek word might well be translated). Matthew expands the descriptions of the 'happy people', as given in Luke—adding *in spirit* to *the poor* (rightly sensing the underlying thought, that poverty must be allied to piety), adding *after righteousness* to *the hungry* and *thirsty* (meaning probably those desiring the longed-for blessing in the coming Kingdom), and adding *for righteousness' sake* to *the persecuted* (making explicit what is implicit in Luke.)

The blessings (particularly in Matt.) are in the future; they are to be realized in the coming Kingdom. *The woes* are found only in Luke. They are the negative side of the teaching of which the beatitudes are the positive.

43. *The influence of salt and light*
Matthew 5: 13–16 Luke 14: 34–35
11: 33

There is a similar saying about salt in Mark 9: 49–50 (Section 90). Matthew here seems to refer to the use of salt for manuring purposes. Luke refers to its use in preserving food. *Savourless salt* is used as a metaphor for the uselessness of the disciple who had lost his fervour. . . . Verse 15 in Matthew (Luke 11: 33) is similar to the parable of the lamp in Section 33.

The elevated character, like *a city set on a hill*, cannot be hidden and Jesus says the true disciple cannot hide his light. The *bushel* was a dry measure, about half a peck. The *stand* was a metal lampstand which supported the earthenware lamp. In Matthew the *lamp* is thought of as illuminating the whole of the Palestinian one-room house, while Luke seems to be thinking of the porch of a Graeco-Roman house, with a niche for a lamp in the wall of the vestibule. Such houses have been unearthed in the ruins of Pompeii.

It has been suggested that Jesus was not speaking here to his disciples but to the Pharisees and other Jews of his day. They were supposed to be salt and light (and so they considered themselves) but they had let their salt become savourless and had hidden their light under a bushel, instead of displaying it to others.

44. *Jesus and the Jewish Law*
Matthew 5: 17–20

This is the introduction to a number of paragraphs in the Sermon on the Mount on the Jewish Law. *The Law and the prophets* means the Hebrew Bible. To *fulfil* means to 'fill' the Law, to realize the full depth of its meaning. Jesus criticized the Law at many points but evidently held that on the whole it was valid.

Verse 18 has a parallel in Luke 16: 17. *Till heaven and earth pass away* means 'until the end of the present age'. The *jot* represents the Hebrew letter *yod*—the smallest character, which can be dispensed with in many Hebrew words. The *tittle* (or horn) is a small projection which distinguishes some Hebrew letters from others, just as the English y is distinguished from v only by a small 'tail'.

Verses 18 and 19 seem strange on the lips of Jesus, for in some cases he did put aside the Jewish Law. It has been suggested that the saying preserved in Mark 13: 31 is the original of this—*my words shall not pass away*—and it has been altered in Matthew into a saying about the eternal validity of the Jewish religion.

There follow five examples of the Jewish Law and Jesus' attitude to the commandments and his application of them: (*a*) On killing and the necessity for reconciliation (verses 21–26); (*b*) on adultery and the necessity for inner purity (27–32); (*c*) on swearing and the necessity for sincerity (33–37); (*d*) on reciprocity in vengeance and the necessity for non-resistance (38–42); (*e*) on loving one's neighbour and the necessity for love for all (43–48).

45. *On murder and reconciliation*

Matthew 5: 21–26 Luke 12: 57–59

Ye have heard that it was said is the introductory formula of each of these instances of teaching about the Law. It may be meant literally, for the people addressed by Jesus had heard the Law read in the synagogue each Sabbath.

Thou shalt not kill comes from the Ten Commandments, the rest of 21 in Matthew comes from the tradition of the elders. Jesus here stresses that what matters so much in not the outward action of murder but the inner thought of anger and hatred. . . . *Raca* is from an Aramaic word meaning 'empty' and is here used as an expression of contempt or abuse. The *Council* is literally the Sanhedrin, which means here either the supreme court at Jerusalem or else the local council which met in connection with the synagogue. . . . *Hell* is a translation of the Greek word *Gehenna*. This was in Hebrew *Ge-Hinnom*—the valley of

Hinnom, a ravine to the west of Jerusalem. Ahaz is said to have practised the fire-worship of the god Molech there. Because of its pagan associations it was defiled by Josiah (see 2 Kings 23: 6, 10, 18) and was later used as a burning place for the rubbish of the city. Because of the fires which were continually burning there, the name became a symbol for the place of future punishment. *Fire* is a metaphor for purification, however, as well as destruction.

Matthew gives two illustrations of the principle Jesus enunciated (23–26). The worshipper in Jerusalem brought his gift to the inner court of the Temple, in which the altar stood. The implication here is that the man offering his gift is in the wrong. Reconciliation in the New Testament is always of the wrong-doer to the righteous one, not the other way round.

Matthew (25–26) is paralleled in Luke 12: 57–59. In Luke it is a picture of crisis, in view of the near approach of the judgment. In Matthew it is an illustration of the law of brotherhood. The word for *officer* in Matthew is an inferior official. Luke uses a different Greek word, which meant in ancient Athens a collector who had to enter as due a fine fixed by the magistrate. Later it meant a court official.

46. *On adultery and divorce*

Matthew 5: 27–32

This is another illustration of the deeper principles of the Jewish Law, as brought out by Jesus. His standard dealt with thoughts and intentions, the Rabbis' decrees dealt with acts.

The warning against offences (28–30) is taken from Mark 9: 43–48 (Section 90). . . . For the term *hell* see the previous section. Jesus here (29–30) adopted the popular Jewish conception of the body being punished in Gehenna.

There are also parallels in other places for 31–32 (see Section 93). Jesus here forbids divorce (except for immorality) and remarriage.

47. *On swearing*
Matthew 5: 33–37

There were Rabbinic discussions held about the lawfulness of oaths. To *forswear thyself* means to swear falsely, to break an oath or commit perjury. This was of course forbidden by the Law. Jesus here points out that oaths are not necessary at all, if a person really means what he says. . . . There is a similar phrase in James 5: 12—*Let your yea be yea and your nay be nay*—and this is perhaps nearer to Jesus' actual words than the version here (37).

48. *On retaliation and loving one's enemies*
Matthew 5: 38–48 Luke 6: 27–36

These are the last two illustrations given in Matthew of Jesus' attitude to the Jewish Law. In Luke the verses about non-retaliation (29–30) are in the middle of the passage about loving one's enemies, while 31 (the Golden Rule) is found later in Matthew 7: 21 (see Section 57).

The law *an eye for an eye and a tooth for a tooth*, was originally restrictive. Among primitive peoples the rule was 'a life for an eye'! This law limited vengeance to compensation for the exact amount of injury received, instead of vengeance unlimited. It was thus an advance on earlier practice. Jesus holds, however, that even this does not go far enough. He takes extreme instances of the way in which his new spirit of forgiveness and love might work out in life (there are parallels in Rom. 12: 17).

The *cloak* is an outer garment, the *coat* an inner one. The former was the more valuable and was an absolute necessity for the poor peasant of Palestine. Matthew depicts legal proceedings in which this has to be surrendered, while Luke pictures a robber as seizing it. . . . The phrase about *going another mile* (41 in Matt.) is a reference to the situation in Palestine under the Romans. A Roman soldier of the army of occupation had the right to make a native of the country carry his pack for a mile. Jesus suggests a man might offer to go another mile after the compulsory one.

On loving one's enemies. Luke (27–28) preserves the rhythmic parallelism of the words of Jesus. *Love* is parallel to *do good*, *bless* parallel to *pray for.* This shows what Jesus meant by love—active goodness in conduct towards one's enemies as well as one's friends. . . . The Old Testament quotation in Matthew (43) refers to the attitude of the Jew towards his fellow-countryman—his *neighbour*. *And hate thine enemy* is not in the Old Testament but was an inference drawn by the Rabbis.

Matthew (46–48) refers to *publicans* and *Gentiles* as instances of those who are outcasts, from the point of view of the strict Jew. *Perfect* (48 in Matt.—but *merciful* in 36 of Luke) means 'fulfilling an end'. The thought seems to be that man should fulfil his function in his own sphere, just as God fulfils his in the eternal sphere, by being kind and loving towards his enemies.

The words *never despairing* in Luke (35) may mean, 'without expecting anything back'. A possible translation, however, is 'despairing of no man', and this seems to reflect better the attitude urged by Jesus.

49. *Almsgiving*
Matthew 6: 1–4

The next portion of the Sermon on the Mount (6: 1–18) deals with three religious practices which were current among the Jews—almsgiving, prayer and fasting. In each case Jesus counsels a more spiritual and a less ostentatious observance. Verse 1 is an introduction to the whole passage. *Do your righteousness* means 'practise your religion'.

Special merit was attached by the Jews to giving alms. But they often did this in the wrong spirit, calling attention to their own generosity. The reference to *sounding a trumpet* is sarcastic—an instance of the humour of Jesus. The word *hypocrite* meant originally an actor. Actors on the Greek stage wore masks, which helped the audience to identify them, before the age of footlights; but it also served to hide their real faces. Thus the word was applied to those who 'played a part', whose actions were not in accord with their true impulses.

50. *Prayer*
Matthew 6: 5–15 Luke 11: 1–4

Standing was the usual Jewish attitude for prayer, in the synagogue or elsewhere. *Use not vain repetitions* probably means 'Do not speak thoughtlessly'. The emphasis is not on the repetition but on the quality of the prayer expressed by the words used.

In Matthew the Lord's Prayer is included here. Luke gives it in another setting. The latter is much shorter and may be nearer the original, for Matthew may have added Jewish expressions and made the prayer more suitable for public use. (The Revised Version correctly gives Luke 11: 2–4. In later manuscripts and versions it was copied out to approximate to the Matt. version.) *Our daily bread* uses a curious Greek word which may mean 'bread for the coming day', 'our needful bread' or 'bread enough for one day.' . . . The petition *Lead us not into temptation* often causes difficulty. Does God do this? We must remember that the Jewish way of thinking dispensed with secondary causes. If God permitted a thing, they said he ordered it. So we might put it here: 'Do not allow us to fall into temptation set by others.' The phrase is parallel to the following one—*Deliver us from evil.*

Matthew adds a warning (14–15) that divine forgiveness is dependent on human forgiveness. If 15 sounds harsh, we must remember that in the divine sphere 'will' is the same as 'can'. Men who do not themselves forgive cannot be forgiven, for they are not willing to accept the forgiveness of God.

51. *Fasting*
Matthew 6: 16–18

Strict Jews fasted on Mondays and Thursdays. Jesus here warns against the wrong spirit in fasting. The *hypocrites* used ashes, or left the beard and hair untended or coloured their faces to make them look pale. In these ways they showed people that they were fasting and very pious. Jesus is surely being ironical in describing such practices as *disfiguring their faces*. On the other hand, *anointing the head* and *washing the face* would suggest the appearance of feasting rather than fasting.

52. *The true treasure*
Matthew 6: 19–21 Luke 12: 33–34

Both versions probably came from Q. Matthew is the more rhythmical here, while Luke includes this in another section of Jesus' teaching.

Rust (19 in Matt.) is literally 'food'. It probably means the devouring by mice, etc., of wealth stored in barns. The thieves *break through* the thin walls of a Palestinian cottage, as indicated in Matthew. Luke thinks rather of a Roman house, to which thieves *draw nigh*.

53. *The single eye*
Matthew 6: 22–24 Luke 11: 34–36
16: 13

Matthew has here brought together two sets of sayings, both of which have the same emphasis. *The eye* was considered as the means whereby light reached the whole body, like the window of a room. If that was obscured, the house was darkened. *Body* here means more than simply the physical; it includes the whole personality. We might paraphrase: 'If your outlook is single and your intention pure, your whole personality will be illumined.'

The second saying has the same point—the necessity for singleness of mind. The statement about *serving two masters* is a paradox, for it is an obvious impossibility. It was perhaps deliberately framed in order to provoke thought. *Mammon* (Luke 16: 13) is a Semitic word meaning 'wealth' or 'gain'.

54. *On anxiety*
Matthew 6: 25–34 Luke 12: 22–32

The beautiful rhythmical structure of this well-known passage is particularly plain in the version in Matthew.

The word translated *stature* (27 in Matt., 25 in Luke) may mean 'height' or 'age'. The word translated *cubit* could mean 'span'. So we might translate here 'add a span to his age'. Some think this the more probable rendering. A cubit (eighteen inches) to the height would be a large addition, not *that which is least* (26 in Luke). The irony of the saying is that worry shortens life instead of lengthening it.

The lilies of the field would include wild flowers generally, such as anemones, poppies and irises. The *oven* is a portable oven. The grass was used as fuel to light the fire underneath. . . The phrase in Luke (29) *neither be of doubtful mind* may mean 'Do not be tossed about' or 'Do not be lifted up'—in suspense. It is a call for decision, since God is Father.

55. *On judging others*
Matthew 7: 1–6 Luke 6: 37–42

The figures of speech in Luke (38) is taken from the practice of measuring grain. A girded upper garment was worn in which bulky things could be carried. This would be held out to contain a full measure of grain, even *running over*.

A vivid picture is given in both Matthew and Luke of a man finding fault with his brother, while his own faults are even more apparent. The *mote* is a twig or splinter, a piece of dried wood or straw. The *beam* is the main beam in the house, which supports the others.

Luke has two verses (39–40) which refer to the

responsibility of the teacher in guiding his pupils. They are paralleled in Matthew 15: 14 and 10: 24–25.

The final statement in Matthew (6) is difficult to reconcile with the spirit and teaching of Jesus and many have considered that it did not come from him at all, but represents the attitude towards 'outsiders' of the strict Jewish Christians. They shrank from letting *dogs* and *swine* share the *pearls* of their faith.

The only other reasonable suggestion seems to be that this verse should be read after the section in Matthew 6: 1–18, which are concerned with the manner in which almsgiving, prayer and fasting should be observed—without ostentation. This verse fitly concludes this topic: 'Do all these things in private, without making a show about them. The crowd would not understand and both you and your religion would suffer. This would be to cast holy things to dogs and pearls to swine.' Even if this is right, it seems a harsh way for Jesus to have expressed himself.

56. *On asking*

Matthew 7: 7–11 Luke 11: 9–13

This paragraph in Luke comes in the middle of a block of teaching about prayer (Luke 11: 1–13). . . . *Bread* and *fish* are common articles of diet in Palestine.

Jesus' argument is an *a fortiori* one, from the character of men and of God. Jesus assumes two things about men—that they are evil, with bad tendencies, and yet they have good in them and give good things to the children whom they love. . . . The phrase in Matthew *good things* (11) is more likely to be original than Luke—*the Holy Spirit* (13). Luke is fond of referring to the Spirit and would interpret Jesus' words as meaning this here.

57. *The Golden Rule*
Matthew 7: 12 Luke 6: 31

In Matthew this is a summary of the spirit of the Old Testament. In Luke it is apparently Jesus' own principle.

This rule was enunciated by the Jewish Rabbis, in a negative form. Hillel said: 'What is hateful to thee, thou shalt not do to thy brother. This is the whole Law and all else is commentary.' It has also been found in non-Christian teachers. Confucius said: 'What you do not want done to yourself, do not to others.' This also is negative.

58. *The narrow way*
Matthew 7: 13–14 Luke 13: 22–24

In Luke this is an utterance of Jesus on the last journey to Jerusalem. There is a sense of urgency, and this situation may account for the stern nature of the saying. . . . Luke speaks of a narrow *door* into a room. Matthew thinks of a city *gate*, through which the road passes.

59. *On fruit and the treasure of the heart*
Matthew 7: 15–20 Luke 6: 43–45

There is a parallel to these sayings in Jesus' defence when he was charged with casting out demons with the help of Beelzebub (Section 28; Matt. 12: 33–35).

The general principle is illustrated here that only good things can produce good results; a good tree produces good fruit and a good man produces good from his heart. The converse is also true of evil things. Verse 19 in Matthew is reminiscent of the teaching of John the Baptist (Matt. 3: 10) and possibly the author has here attributed it wrongly to Jesus.

60. *The confession of lordship. The parable of the two foundations*

Matthew 7: 21–29 — Luke 6: 46–49; 13: 25–27

The Sermon in both Matthew and Luke concludes with statements about the necessity for practising Jesus' teaching—doing the things he says, and not simply listening to them. Matthew adds (22–23) a section found in Luke 13: 25–27. In Luke, however, those who ask for admission (into the Kingdom) base their claim on the fact that they have shared Jesus' life and heard his teaching, i.e., that they are Jews. In Matthew they say that they have prophesied and worked miracles in his name, i.e., they are Christian teachers. Both are alike rejected because their actions do not come up to their profession.

This is enforced by the parable of the two foundations. The true foundation, which enables a house to stand in the storms, is the practice of Jesus' teaching as enunciated in the Sermon. Matthew speaks of two men building houses in different places—one on the rock and the other on earth and sand. The foresight of the first builder is stressed, in choosing the right place to build. A river torrent filled the dry sandy bed when the rainy season came and the second house collapsed. In Luke the stress is on the diligence of the wise builder, who dug deep until he came to the rock beneath the loose earth. The foolish man built on the upper stratum without troubling to dig down to a foundation.

The version in Matthew seems to reflect the conditions in Palestine more faithfully. The narrow wadi becomes a roaring torrent when the rain and wind and floods come. Luke seems rather to be thinking of the broad rivers of Syria, which rise in flood. Matthew reproduces the Semitic parallelism; the paragraph is really a poem of two stanzas. The parallel is perfect, as far as the sudden break into prose in the last line.

Matthew concludes his three chapters with 28—his usual formula at the end of a discourse of Jesus—and 29, which is taken from the account in Mark 1: 22 of the effect of Jesus' first preaching in Capernaum.

(*f*) Further Galilaean Activities

61. *The healing of the centurion's servant*

Matthew 8: 5–13 Luke 7: 1–10
13: 28–30

This is one of the few incidents in the Gospels where Jesus had dealings with Gentiles. The centurion was apparently a Roman and was one of the class known as 'God-fearers'—Gentiles who were attracted by the Jewish worship of one God and attended the synagogue, but did not accept the Jewish Law and its obligations.

The centurion's plea is marked by his humility. In Matthew he comes himself to Jesus, whereas in Luke he approaches him through two different embassies. In Matthew the sick person is the centurion's 'boy', which may mean either his son or his servant. In Luke it is his slave. . . . Jesus praised the confidence of the centurion in him and his powers by saying that this was greater faith than he had found among the Jews.

Matthew adds a saying (11–12) which is found in another context in Luke 13. It denotes a wider conception of the Kingdom of God than the national one current among most Jews in Jesus' day. The Kingdom is here pictured as a banquet—a familiar Jewish figure. Those who come 'recline' in the Kingdom, as at a meal, while those who expected to be present are outside the well-lit room, in the outer darkness. The rejected ones are presumably Jews—*the sons of the Kingdom* (Matthew). Jesus evidently thought of the Kingdom as not restricted to one nation or as being open to any by national right. . . . The phrase in Matthew *the weeping and the gnashing of teeth*, is a conventional formula found elsewhere in this Gospel (24: 51, 25: 30).

62. *The widow's son at Nain*

Luke 7: 11–17

The site of Nain is unknown, as the place is not mentioned elsewhere in the Bible and is not found in Josephus. Luke emphasizes that the boy was the only son of a widow—a typical note. In *touching the bier* Jesus showed that he disregarded the ritual uncleanness which was held to be incurred by touching something belonging to a dead body. Some people think the boy was not actually dead, but in a state of coma; in this case there would be no objection to Jesus' touching him or the bier.

This miracle is somewhat remarkable in that there is no mention of the faith of anyone. The cure seems to have been wrought by Jesus out of pure compassion.

63. *The anointing in Simon's house*

Luke 7: 36–50

This is a different episode from that given in Section 154, from Mark and Matthew. At Bethany, just before the Passion, a woman anointed Jesus' head, as a sign of honour. Here a woman who was a notorious sinner anointed Jesus' feet, to supply the courtesies usual to a guest in the East. A curious point of resemblance is that the host of Jesus was called Simon in both cases—a common Jewish name. In Luke he is a Pharisee (44), while in Mark 14 the incident takes place in the house of Simon the leper.

In the East the door to the street or the courtyard is open during a meal; hence the entry of the woman into the room. The Pharisee seems to have invited Jesus in a spirit of condescension, for he omitted the usual courtesy (44) and criticized Jesus under his breath (39). His assumption is that if Jesus had been a prophet with the prophet's usual insight into human character, he would have driven the woman off.

The connection between the parable of the two debtors and Jesus' remarks to the woman is not very close, although there is a common underlying idea. It is that the real basis of forgiveness is love and the spring of love should be a sense of forgiveness. The debtors who were forgiven loved as a consequence. The woman was forgiven because she loved. The two thoughts are combined in 47 . . . As in a previous incident (Section 21), complaint was made that Jesus forgave sins (50), although in both instances Jesus actually had declared the person's sins forgiven, i.e. by God.

64. *The women who ministered to Jesus*

Luke 8: 1–3

Mark also mentions, quite incidentally, the presence of women who served Jesus in Galilee, when narrating the crucifixion (Mark 15: 40–41). . . . Mary Magdalene is mentioned here for the first time. Here trouble was not moral; the possession of *seven demons* does not mean that she was a bad woman. It was probably mental trouble—perhaps a form of hysteria. Joanna is not mentioned elsewhere. Her husband was probably steward to Herod Antipas, as the setting is still in Galilee. Susanna was evidently well-known, as no further description is given of her.

65. *The storm on the lake*

Matthew 8: 23–27 Mark 4: 35–41 Luke 8: 22–25

The narrative in Mark follows on Jesus' teaching from a boat (4: 1). *The other side* of the lake presumably means the eastern shore, for the company arrive there in the following paragraph. Sudden storms are common on the Lake of Galilee, owing to the geographical situation. The hot air rises from the lake and the plain, which is nearly 700 feet below sea level. Then cold air rushes in through the ravines on the north-east to take its place and the waters of the comparatively narrow lake are wildly stirred. Storms in Galilee cease as suddenly as they begin.

Both Matthew and Luke tone down the vivid account in Mark. The disciples' rebuke to Jesus *Rabbi, carest thou not that we perish?* becomes in Matthew *Save, Lord, we perish*, and in Luke *Master, master, we perish*. Matthew omits the rebuke to the disciples and the great fear which came upon them. . . . This is one of the few nature-miracles in the Gospels—stories which suggest that Jesus had command over the forces of nature. The words of command by Jesus are literally: 'Keep silent! But muzzled!', as if he were speaking to a person. Some have thought of a 'demon' of the storm and many consider that Jesus was stilling the elements. Others, however, suggest that the words are more appropriate if addressed to the frightened disciples (or to the one who woke him, as the verbs are singular), who were putting the boat in peril by their panic.

66. *The madman of the Gerasenes*
Matthew 8: 28–34   Mark 5: 1–20   Luke 8: 26–39

The account in Mark is particularly vivid and is closely followed by Luke. Matthew, however, considerably abbreviates and strangely mentions two madmen (see Section 131 for another case where this writer duplicates people who are cured). Perhaps he assumed, from the mention of a legion of demons, that there was more than one possessed man.

The land indicated is the eastern border of the Lake of Galilee. The correct rendering in Mark and Luke is probably Gerasenes (the Greek manuscripts differ), while Matthew has Gadarenes. . . . Mark gives a good description of the terrors of madness and the strength of the madman. Such men were popularly thought in the first century to be possessed by *demons*. (Here and elsewhere this is the more correct term, rather than *devils*. Another Greek word would be used for that. There was considered to be one devil, but numberless demons.) The *tombs* would be caves on the hillside, where the dead were buried. As nobody would go near such a place, the man would be safe there.

The man's salutation to Jesus—*Son of the Most High God*—may mean the Messiah. But the man may have been a Gentile, since this part of Palestine was largely Gentile (witness the keeping of a herd of pigs) and he may have been expressing his feeling that Jesus came from the Jewish God. Jesus asked *What is thy name?* It was a current practice for an exorcist (one who sought to drive out demons) to ask the name of the demon, so as to get power over it. Jesus may have been using this idea; or he may have been calling the man to realize that the demons possessing him were not his real personality. *Legion* was a Latin word and meant a division in the Roman army—normally about five thousand men.

In Mark (and Luke) Jesus' part is only permissive. He does not order the demons into the swine but only allows them to go. Probably the pigs were being neglected by the swineherds, who wanted to see and hear what was going on. Then the pigs went too near the cliff, took panic and plunged over the edge. The belief that the demons had left the man and gone into the pigs (since popular thought declared that demons had to inhabit some body, human or animal) was the 'explanation' given afterwards for the loss of the pigs.

Jesus broke here his usual rule, which was to enjoin silence on people who were cured. Perhaps the danger accompanying his cures becoming known was not so great in this district, as Jesus was not living there. *Decapolis* (20 in Mark) means literally 'ten cities' and was the name of a district east of the Jordan.

67. *Jairus' daughter and the woman with haemorrhage*

Matthew 9: 18–26 <u>Mark 5: 21–43</u> Luke 8: 40–56

Both Matthew and Luke considerably abbreviate Mark here. In all three Gospels the story of the woman's cure is dovetailed into the account of Jairus' daughter.

Jairus was *a ruler of the synagogue*, i.e. one of the elders attached to the synagogue. They had the arranging of public worship in their hands and formed a kind of committee of management. Jairus was not a priest, since these did not officiate in the synagogue. The *border* of Jesus' garment, which Matthew and Luke both mention, was the tassel which hung from the edge of a Jew's robe.

When Jesus arrived at Jairus' house, the preparations for mourning had already begun, with the weeping and wailing usual on such occasions. The only evidence that the girl was dead is the message brought to Jairus. Against this is Jesus' own statement that she was asleep and not dead. The Gospel writers probably understood this as referring to the 'sleep of death', but a Greek word is used here different from the usual word for this and such a meaning would hardly have point here. The people in the house evidently took Jesus to mean the girl was still alive—perhaps in a sleep or coma.

The actual Aramaic words of Jesus are preserved—*Talitha cumi*—although the account was written in Greek (cf. Mark 7: 34, 14: 36, 15: 34). Early Christians would greatly value such phrases. The usual English translation is too stiff. It is an affectionate phrase—literally 'Little lamb, get up'.

68. *The healing of two blind men*
Matthew 9: 27–31

This is found only in Matthew and is like the story of Bartimaeus (Section 131)—cf. the cry of the blind men, Jesus' question to them and the reference to their faith. The means employed by Jesus—touching the man's eyes—is used also in the story of a blind man in Mark (Section 82). As with the case of the leper (Section 20), Jesus strictly charged the man not to make his cure known, but was disobeyed.

69. *The healing of a dumb demoniac*
Matthew 9: 32–34

This is reminiscent of the cure of a dumb man (Luke 11: 14)—blind and dumb, according to Matthew (12: 22). As here, people marvelled at this, but others said that Jesus was using the power of Beelzebub to cast out demons (see Section 28). This is thought by most critics to be the same occasion, told once again by Matthew.

70. *The rejection of Jesus at Nazareth*
Matthew 13: 53–58 Mark 6: 1–6a Luke 4: 16–30

Mark and Matthew do not actually mention Nazareth, although this is obviously the place intended. Luke seems to have an independent account, although no doubt it refers to the same occasion.

The statement in Mark of the people *Is not this the carpenter?* is our authority for thinking that Jesus himself carried on Joseph's trade, although this is in itself most probable. This is also the only place where the names of Jesus' brothers are given and where mention is made of the fact that he had sisters also (see Section 28 for another mention of his brothers). James became the leader of the Church in Jerusalem after the crucifixion; Judas (or Jude) also joined the Church. Nothing is known of the other brothers or of his sisters.

The conclusion in Mark (5) is very blunt—Jesus could do nothing at Nazareth, because of the people's lack of confidence in him. Jesus was surprised to find this. Matthew changes this to say that Jesus *did* not do *many* mighty works there, and he omits mention of Jesus' surprise.

In Luke, Jesus reads from Isaiah 61: 1. This passage

from the writings contained in 'Isaiah' recalls the Servant Poems of Deutero-Isaiah. The prophet was of course referring to his own inspiration, not to a coming Messiah. Jesus appropriated the prophet's words to himself. . . . After the reading in the synagogue the reader or another gave an address, for which he was seated. Jesus' words are probably summarized in 21. On the complaint of the people Jesus quoted two proverbs—about a doctor and about the reception of a prophet in his own country (cf. Mark 6: 4). He showed from the Old Testament itself that some of their own prophets had not confined their mission to Jews. He may have been suggesting that his own ministry was not only for his fellow-countrymen, or at any rate not simply for the people of Nazareth.

The synagogue service was broken up (29). The last statement in Luke means either that Jesus escaped or that the people realized the danger of what they were trying to do and let him go. There is no record in the Gospels of any visit to Nazareth after this.

71. *The mission of the twelve disciples*

Matthew 10: 5–42 Mark 6: 6b–13 Luke 9: 1–6

Luke here follows Mark. Matthew, however, has produced a long discourse of Jesus, using Mark and other material—from the document Q and his own special matter.

The wandering preacher would be a familiar figure to Jesus' contemporaries. Preachers or teachers would carry a staff and a wallet and only such provisions as they needed for their journey to the next town or village. The disciples of Jesus are here forbidden to take luggage, for they were apparently only on a short tour; they were not to take a *wallet*—the word used means a beggar's bag for money to be put in. They were to accept hospitality, but were to reject any place which would not receive them. To *shake off the dust* of one's feet was a symbolic gesture meaning 'We have nothing to do with you now'. The disciples preached repentance, exorcised possessed people and anointed the sick with oil—a practice among doctors in the East. Luke adds that they preached the Kingdom of God (2).

The version in Matthew of the instructions to the disciples is in three parts: (*a*) 5–15 seem to apply to a short journey of the apostles around Galilee; (*b*) 16–23 are applicable rather to the circumstances of the Church after the time of Jesus; (*c*) 24–42 are general instructions to preachers, given by Jesus on different occasions.

Verses 5–15 are similar in Mark, with additions. The disciples are here expressly told not to go to Samaria or to Gentile countries. . . . Sodom and Gemorrah were the typical cities of wickedness. Sodom is also cited as a city which insulted its guests (see also Section 101).

Verses 16–23 suggest later conditions. The Acts records how disciples were brought before rulers and punished. *Councils* is literally Sanhedrins; local synagogues had the right of judging and punishing offenders. In 19–20 Jesus does not deprecate all preparation for public speaking. If the disciples were suddenly arrested, however, they would not have time to prepare a public defence. Jesus tells them that if their minds are full of the things they have been taught, the Holy Spirit will prompt them what to say. . . . Much of this paragraph is found in Mark 13: 9–13 (Section 147), where it seems more appropriate. Some have thought that the reference to the coming of the Son of Man in 23 means simply that Jesus would follow his disciples and overtake them on their journey before they have completed their circuit. Others suggest that the phrase really comes from the writer, who was seeking to assure the Christian missionaries of his own time that Jesus would return before they had finished their task.

Verses 24–42 relate to various topics. Jesus encourages the disciples (24–25), speaks on the necessity to proclaim his message (26–27), on the care of God (28–31), on confessing him (32–33), on the results of his coming among men (34–39), and on the reception of his disciples (40–42). . . . The one whom we are to fear (28) is taken by some to be the evil one, by others to be God. On *Gehenna* see note in Section 45. To *confess* (32) means to acknowledge. Jesus means (in 34) that the *result* of his coming will be that people from the same household will be divided against each other. It does not of course mean that he countenanced war on his behalf. Verse 38 is a grim metaphor, for in Roman times the man carrying a cross through the streets was on his way to execution.

Matthew 11: 1 really belongs to this section. It is the usual formula in Matthew for concluding one of the discourses of Jesus.

72. *Herod's opinion of Jesus*

Matthew 14: 1–2 <u>Mark 6: 14–16</u> Luke 9: 7–9

Another statement of Herod's attitude towards Jesus is in Luke 13: 31 (Section 117). Herod Antipas is called *king* in Mark. This was a courtesy title; his correct one was *tetrarch*, as Matthew and Luke give.

The translation of the verb in 14 of Mark is uncertain—*he said* (i.e. Herod) or *they said* (i.e. people were saying). Similar ideas about Jesus on the part of the people are recorded by the disciples at Caesarea Philippi (Section 83). Herod's own opinion is given in 16. By saying that Jesus was John people may have meant simply that Jesus in his teaching and spirit was 'like John all over again'.

73. *The question of John from prison*

Matthew 11: 2–19 Luke 7: 18–35

This section is put here so that all the information about John and his imprisonment may be brought together (Sections 72–74). Luke 3: 19–20 gives a statement about his imprisonment by Herod Antipas. The Jewish historian, Josephus, says that John was in the fortress of Machaerus, on the eastern shore of the Dead Sea. This was in territory ruled by Herod. According to Matthew and Luke his friends were allowed access to him. John's question to Jesus is generally taken as indicating doubt on the part of John, as Jesus' mode of living was so different from that of John himself when he was free. But it is possible that the news of Jesus' work roused in John not doubt but hope. He began to wonder if he had not been a failure after all and was to have a successor, as he had predicted. Jesus was, however, different from what he had imagined, so he sent his disciples to make sure.

The question *Art thou he that cometh?* is generally taken to mean the Messiah. It is possible John meant 'Is this Elijah?', since Elijah was popularly regarded as the one to come before the advent of the Kingdom of God. . . . Jesus' reply referred John's messengers to the work he was doing. The sayings are based on Isaiah 35: 5 and 61: 1. They conclude with a message of encouragement to John.

Jesus continued, by giving his opinion of John. The words *a reed waving in the wind* and *a man with fine clothes* are of course ironical. John was certainly not like that! The one who is *but little in the Kingdom of God* is generally regarded as meaning the humblest Christian.

Verses 12–13 in Matthew are found in Luke 16: 16 (Section 124). The meaning is perhaps that *men of violence* such as Zealots, tax-collectors and sinners were forcing themselves into the Kingdom and were welcomed by Jesus. Others think it is a condemnation of such men of violence, who would seek to bring in the Kingdom by force.

The last section (15–18 in Matt., 31–35 in Luke) is a parable about children's games. This may be a reminiscence of Jesus' boyhood. It is not an exact analogy but a general description of the Jews of the time. They were like sulky children, who refuse to join in whatever game their companions suggest—whether funerals or weddings!

The final comment (*works* in Matt., *children* in Luke) is a proverbial saying, the meaning of which is not quite clear. Matthew means: 'Those who follow wisdom show this by their works, the results they produce.' Luke may mean: 'The wisdom of God is justified by her children, i.e. those who listen to Jesus and John.'

74. *The death of John the Baptist*
Matthew 14: 3–12 Mark 6: 17–29

The account in Josephus of the circumstances of John's imprisonment is mentioned in Section 73. The story of his death is not, however, found elsewhere than here.

John's rebuke to Herod was based on the Old Testament law (Lev. 18: 16, 20: 21), which stated that a man might not marry his brother's wife during his brother's lifetime. Herod had also broken another law in marrying Herodias, for she was his niece (and also the niece of her first husband). He also divorced his first wife in favour of Herodias. Herodias and Philip had a daughter named Salome, who is the dancer mentioned here. She would be a girl of twelve or fifteen at this time. Herod was apparently adopting the Roman fashion of interspersing the courses of a meal with entertainment. This was usually by slaves and it would be an extremely undignified thing for a young princess to dance before the guests. The *lords and high captains* (21 in Mark) who were present would be officers in Herod's army.

The statement that Herod *would not reject her* (26 in Mark) means he did not wish to break faith with her. For the sake of foolish consistency and for fear of the scorn of his courtiers, he was willing to do a shameful deed. The *charger* was a dish or platter—probably suggested to Herodias by the sight of the dishes going into the banquet.

75. *The return of the twelve disciples. The feeding of the five thousand.*

Matthew 14: 13–21 <u>Mark 6: 30–44</u> Luke 9: 10–17

On the return of the disciples (Section 71), Jesus apparently desired a period of quiet with them, so he sought to withdraw from the crowds in the neighbourhood of Capernaum. The site of the *desert place* to which they went is uncertain. It evidently could be reached either by boat or on foot, by going round the shore of the lake. It may have been to the south-west of the lake or to the north—at any rate within walking distances of Capernaum. The remark of the disciples, *The place is desert* means simply that it was open country, with no large towns near. There were villages and small farms about, however.

The *penny* was a *denarius*—a silver Roman coin which was a day's wage for a labourer. Dictionaries often give its equivalent as $9\frac{1}{2}d.$ but twice as many shillings would be nearer its equivalent now. . . . Only Mark (39) gives the vivid touch about the *green grass*. This shows the time was spring. The blessing Jesus gave before distributing the bread was the usual action of the host at a meal.

Some think of Jesus as multiplying loaves and fish to make enough to satisfy this large crowd. Others, however, point out that no crowd in the East would go into the country without taking provisions. The Jews always took their own food with them, as this had to be especially prepared. They carried it in small baskets on their shoulders; a Roman referred scornfully to the Jew as 'the man with the basket'. It is also unlikely that the crowd would all have finished their provisions earlier in the day, without keeping some for an evening meal. The disciples themselves appear to have had five loaves and two fishes—enough for a light meal for them. It is possible then that Jesus got the disciples, after arranging the crowd in groups, to go and tell the people to share their provisions. Then there was not only enough to go round but some to spare.

In the Temptation, Jesus refused to use his power to produce material food, knowing this was not the way to do his Messianic work. If Jesus here exercised his influence over the crowd to get them to share, this was a true 'miracle'. As the story was told, however, it appeared that the food provided by the disciples sufficed for all the people present.

76. *The journey across the lake*
Matthew 14: 22–36 Mark 6: 45–56

Luke reproduces nothing from Mark now, between 6: 45 and 8: 27. This story is the sequel to the previous one; Jesus wished to return to Bethsaida (see Section 82).

Where the boat was—*in the midst of the sea*—may mean no more than a good way across the lake. After their previous experience in crossing (Section 65), the disciples would try to keep close to the shore. The *fourth watch of the night* was about 3 a.m. The Romans reckoned the time of the night by four watches, the Jews by three. The fourth watch lasted from 3 to 6 a.m. The phrase translated *walking on the water* in Greek may also be rendered 'walking by the water', i.e. on the shore.

Matthew omits the amazement of the disciples (51 in Mark) and substitutes a statement to the opposite effect—that they recognized him as Son of God (33). He adds an account of Peter's attempt to walk across the water (28–31), where he naturally floundered until Jesus supported him back to the boat. This suggests the water was shallow.

Some think that Jesus was able to overcome natural forces and come to the disciples across the lake. Others suggest that the disciples in the boat were not so far from the shore as they imagined and that Jesus, on the shore or in the shallow water, was able to step into the boat. In the half light of the early dawn there would be considerable confusion, as is evidenced by the statement that the disciples at first thought they saw an apparition. Our judgment will ultimately depend on whether we think such an action as is here told of Jesus was worthy of him or not.

The incident is followed by a general statement of Jesus' popularity and his acts of healing at Gennesaret. This was a plain south of Capernaum.

77. *Jesus and scribal tradition*
Matthew 15: 1–20 Mark 7: 1–23

There are three replies of Jesus here to various people about the value of scribal tradition. In 6–8 and 9–13 in Mark he speaks to the Pharisees who had made the complaint against his disciples, in 14–15 he develops his teaching to the multitude and in 18–23 he explains this further to the disciples.

Verses 3–4 in Mark are an editorial explanation, for the sake of Gentile readers, of the ceremonial observances of the Pharisees, although this statement that *all the Jews* did these things is an exaggeration. *Defiled* or *unwashed hands* means strictly secular or profane, as opposed to holy or consecrated. Because they might have had contact with Gentiles and other people outside the Law, the strict Pharisees took particular care to wash their hands ceremonially. This special washing is referred to in the word translated *diligently* (3 in Mark), the meaning of which is uncertain (see Revised Version margin: *up to the elbow*, or, *with the fist*). The *cups* were drinking-vessels, the *pots* were pint pots or pitchers. Even today the strict Jew has his own special household utensils and will not have his food cooked in a vessel belonging to a Gentile.

The *traditions of the elders* were the rules which the scribes had transmitted. They were additions to the written books of the Old Testament. It was believed that these had been handed down from the earliest times and they constituted the 'oral Law', as contrasted with the written Law of Moses. The scribes sought to include the whole range of human conduct in the regulations of the Law and to give guidance for every possible situation in which a Jew might find himself. This resulted in a vast increase in the number of rules binding on a strict Jew.

Corban (11 in Mark: cf. 5 in Matt.) is an Aramaic term meaning a 'gift'. The reference is usually taken to mean that a man might give something to the Temple and then consider himself relieved of the duty of supporting his parents. There is, however, also evidence that *Corban* was a form of Jewish oath. A man might swear that his property was Corban—dedicated—or even say it in a fit of temper; according to the Law he must keep his oath at all costs and he was then not allowed to touch the money in order to help his parents. Jesus points out that the command to honour one's parents is nullified by this practice.

The rest of the paragraph is a return to the original topic and an explanation of true purity. This depends, says Jesus, not on what a man eats but on what kind of thoughts he has (13–15 in Matt. are added from another source). The remark *making all meats clean* (19 in Mark) is a comment of the writer, applying Jesus' argument to the question of the Jewish food-laws, for the benefit of his Gentile readers.

III. JOURNEYS IN THE NORTH

(*a*) Phoenicia and Other Places Outside Galilee

78. *Tyre and Sidon: the Syro-Phoenician woman's daughter*
Matthew 15: 21–28 Mark 7: 24–30

Tyre and Sidon, both of them seaports, were the chief towns of the country of Phoenicia. This was part of the Roman province of Syria, but as an independent country it had had a long history. In the ninth century B.C. Jezebel, daughter of the king of Tyre, married Ahab of Israel, with disastrous consequences for the Hebrews. The Phoenicians were a great colonizing and trading people. They founded the colony of Carthage in North Africa, the great rival of early Rome, settled in Spain and traded with the Britons in Cornwall.

This is the only occasion in which Jesus is known to have gone to a foreign country. He appears to have wished to have a time of quiet with his disciples. . . . The woman is called in Mark *a Greek* because of her language and probably her religion. Mark means she was a Gentile. She was *a Syro-Phoenician* because her race was Phoenician and politically she lived in the province of Syria. Matthew calls her a *Canaanitish* woman, i.e. a descendant of the old inhabitants of Canaan. He does not like to think of Jesus as going into the house in Gentile country, as Mark says (24), so he says the woman *came out* to meet him (22).

Matthew also says that Jesus responded first with silence and gave his disciples his answer (24), suggesting he dealt reluctantly with the woman herself. Mark has nothing of this. The saying about *the dogs* seems strange. The Jews called the Gentiles 'dogs', meaning the unclean pariah or street dogs of the East. They themselves were the 'children'. There were two Greek words for 'dogs', however, and the one used here by Jesus is a diminutive, meaning a domesticated dog. Hence the woman retorted that the dogs eat the crumbs under the tables. In Mark Jesus praises the woman's wit (29). Matthew, more conventionally, makes Jesus commend her faith (28).

79. *Decapolis: the healing of a deaf stammerer*

Mark 7: 31–37

This is one of the two healing stories told only by Mark (see Section 82).

The journey depicted in 31 is a roundabout and indeed extraordinary route. For Decapolis, see Section 66. . . . The phrase in 32 *an impediment in his speech*, is literally 'hardly able to speak', i.e. 'speaking with difficulty'. Possibly the man was dumb. Spittle (33) was considered in the ancient world to have healing properties. Here (and in the story in Section 82) Jesus used a conventional method of healing. Mark gives again the Aramaic term used by Jesus—*Ephphatha*—(cf. Mark 5: 41) and there follows the usual injunction to silence.

80. *The feeding of the four thousand*

Matthew 15: 29–39 Mark 8: 1–10

This is generally regarded today as a duplicate of the story of the feeding of the five thousand, i.e. the same incident, told twice. Mark may have received the two accounts from different sources—perhaps one was written and the other oral. The first story, about the five thousand, is full of vivid and dramatic touches, while the account here is brief and more bare. It opens with only a vague reference to the situation, and the questions of the disciples and of Jesus about provision for the crowd are practically the same as in the previous story. It seems incredible that the disciples should not have remembered, if the same thing had happened before. The only way in which the two stories differ is in the number of the loaves and fishes and the number of the people—details which would naturally vary when a narrative was told or written down by different people independently.

See Section 75 for a discussion of the actual situation. . . . The place mentioned at the end of the account is unknown. Neither Dalmanutha (Mark) or Magadan (Matt.) can be identified.

81. *The Pharisees' demand for a sign*
Matthew 16: 1–12   Mark 8: 11–21

There was also an account of this incident in the document Q (see Section 108). For verses 2–3 of Matthew see Section 114.

By *a sign* Jesus' opponents probably meant something which would be indisputable evidence of his authority. Perhaps they also thought of the 'signs of the times' which were popularly supposed to herald the coming of the Messiah. Jesus had proclaimed the Kingdom of God. Would he substantiate his claim with some supernatural miracle?

In Mark Jesus bluntly refuses to give any sign. In Matthew he says that the only one shall be *the sign of Jonah.* Jonah was an Old Testament prophet of whom the story was told that he was commissioned to go and preach to the heathen people of Nineveh, the capital of the Assyrian Empire. The phrase here probably means 'the sign of a man preaching'; that should be sufficient for the Jews of Jesus' day, as it was sufficient for the Assyrians of Jonah's time, for they repented.

Then there comes one of the most perplexing passages in the Gospels (14–21 in Mark; 5–12 in Matt.). *Leaven* is a metaphor for bad influence (cf. Luke 12: 1). Mark says this refers to the Pharisees and Herod. Matthew says Pharisees and Sadducees; he is fond of putting the two sects together, in spite of their great differences. The remainder of the paragraph seems to consist of a number of sayings brought together by Mark. The disciples misunderstood the metaphor and thought of material food. Jesus' rebuke is a kind of paraphrase of the passage from Isaiah 6 which was quoted in Mark 4: 11–12. The reference to the two feedings (19–21 in Mark; 9–10 in Matt.) is probably distinct from the preceding verses. Since the two stories of the feedings are probably variants of the same incident, these verses would represent the thoughts of Mark, as he sought to make Jesus' meaning clear to his readers.

(*b*) Herod Philip's Territory

82. *The healing of a blind man at Bethsaida*
Mark 8: 22–26

Bethsaida Julius was in the territory ruled by Herod Philip, one of the sons of Herod the Great (see p. 14). It was just off the north-east shore of the Lake of Galilee. It was called Julius in honour of Julia, daughter of the Emperor Augustus.

This and the story in Section 79 are the only two healing acts found only in Mark. Here also Jesus made use of spittle and took the man aside from the crowd. A peculiarity here is that the man's sight was not restored immediately but gradually. . . . The man's remark (24) probably meant: 'I see things which look like trees (which he would know from the feel); but since they walk, they must be men.' The last command of Jesus is different in some manuscripts: either, 'Do not even enter the village', or, 'Do not tell it even in the village'.

83. *Caesarea Philippi*

Matthew 16: 13–28 Mark 8: 27–9: 1 Luke 9: 18–27

This incident marks a turning-point in the ministry of Jesus, in the Synoptic Gospels. It is important for these reasons.

(i) For the first time somebody called Jesus the Messiah. This marks a step forward in the education of the disciples, for Jesus was obviously not like the expected Messiah; Peter's answer to Jesus' second question showed that he at any rate was able to think of a different Messiah from the popular one.

(ii) Jesus immediately began to teach about suffering and death. This brought forth a protest from Peter—again probably voicing the thoughts of the other eleven.

(iii) Jesus now used the term Son of Man. This was associated with ideas of power and glory, but Jesus used it to speak of service and sacrifice.

(iv) Most of Jesus' teaching was now given to the twelve disciples. When he did speak to the crowd it was to call them to sacrifice in his service and taking up a cross.

Caesarea Philippi was to the north-north-east of the lake. It was a recent Greek city, called after Augustus Caesar, in whose honour a temple had been built by Herod the Great, and Philip himself.

The ideas of the people about Jesus, as reported by the disciples, are significant. Elijah was popularly supposed to be coming before the establishment of the Kingdom of God. Matthew adds Jeremiah—presumably because he also had to suffer for the sake of his message. Mark gives the shortest and probably the correct form of Peter's answer—'You are the Messiah'. Luke and Matthew add explanatory words to this.

Matthew adds 17–19. Peter is pronounced blessed. There is a play on his name, which means a *rock*. 'Thou art *Petros* [Aramaic *Kephas*] and on this *petra* [Aramaic *kepha*] I will build my Church', cf. the French *Pierre*. This is a very controversial passage and different views are possible: (i) the Roman Catholic—that the words were addressed to Peter as an individual, appointing him as Jesus' successor; (ii) that the rock was Jesus himself; (iii) that the rock was the acknowledgment of Jesus' Messiahship; (iv) that the rock was the new character which Peter was developing. He had become the sort of person on whom Jesus could rely, as a foundation on which to build.

The word *Church* comes in the Gospels only here and in Matthew 18: 17. *Hades* means death generally, not the abode of evil powers. The metaphor in *gates of Hades* suggests a city, with all its strength. *The keys of the Kingdom of Heaven* are the symbol of rule and authority in the Kingdom of God. *Binding* and *loosing* in Jewish legal phraseology were technical terms for the verdict of a teacher of the Law who declared some action forbidden or permitted. This saying would thus seem to speak of Peter's delivering verdicts—applying the teaching of Jesus, for instance, to the circumstances of the early Church. Possibly the authority given to Peter in 'the keys' was the authority to preach the Kingdom of God and so to influence others that they might enter the Kingdom. There is no warrant here for the popular idea of Peter as holding the door of 'Heaven'.

Teaching to the multitude follows (34 in Mark). Warnings about saving one's life and so losing it and about taking up a cross were also in Q (see Matt. 10: 38–39; Luke 14: 27; 17: 33). . . . Jesus then refers to the popular conception of the coming of the Son of Man in glory *with the holy angels*. This is thought of as in that generation. The final sentence in Mark (9: 1) is a strange statement, altered by the other two writers. Luke omitted the words *come with power*, as the simplest way out. Matthew interpreted it to mean the coming of the Son of Man. The prediction in Mark has been taken to refer to the Transfiguration, the Resurrection, the coming of the Spirit at Pentecost, the destruction of Jerusalem, the spread of the Gospel in the first century. Some of these are rather doubtful as manifestations of the Kingdom of God in that generation. C. H. Dodd translates: '. . . until they have seen that the Kingdom of God has come with power', i.e. some of those present would realize that the Kingdom had already come. Others think the verse is a later addition of a Christian preacher, assuring his hearers that the Kingdom would come in their own lifetime.

In the Synoptics Jesus three times predicts his Passion at Jerusalem—here and in Sections 86 and 97. In each case the statement is very explicit—about his sufferings, rejection by the leaders of the Jews or the Sanhedrin and his death. It is very likely that Jesus did see, especially towards the end of his public ministry, where the opposition of his enemies would lead and realised the danger he was running in going to Jerusalem. So he warned his disciples in advance. But the terms employed in the Gospels probably owe something to the events as they actually happened. Jesus' warnings would be in more general terms.

Each of the statements concludes with a prediction of a rising again *after three days*. Some scholars think it unlikely that Jesus said this in such explicit terms, since the disciples were so unprepared for a resurrection and so unbelieving when Jesus did appear to them again after the crucifixion. *Three days* is a phrase meaning a very short time and probably it represents Jesus' assurance that, in spite of apparent failure, he would be triumphant.

84. *The transfiguration of Jesus*

Matthew 17: 1–13 Mark 9: 2–13 Luke 9: 28–36

The *high mountain* to which Jesus and the three disciples went has been taken as Mount Hermon, about fourteen miles north of Caesarea Philippi. Mount Tabor, in Galilee, has also been suggested.

Moses and Elijah were the great heroes of old and were held to represent the Law and the Prophets respectively. Their appearance here means that the disciples realized that Jesus was in harmony with the Old Testament religion. But their attention was drawn away from these figures to that of Jesus himself; him only were they to hear henceforth. Another suggestion is that the vision represents the three disciples' realization of the truth of Jesus' words about his way being that of suffering. Both Moses and Elijah had suffered much at the hands of their contemporaries, and this experience told them that even the Messiah was to go the same way. Luke seems to support this in his statement that the two men spoke of *his decease which he was about to accomplish at Jerusalem.* The word means literally 'exodus' or departure and is generally taken to refer to Jesus' death. Luke also adds that Jesus was praying and that the eyes of the disciples were heavy with sleep.

Peter's remark shows his impetuous nature. He suggested making *three tabernacles* (i.e. booths or tents) so that they might remain there together. The words of the voice from the cloud are reminiscent of the voice heard by Jesus at his baptism, with the addition: *Hear ye him.*

The following paragraph in Mark (9–13) and Matthew (9–13) is omitted by Luke. The teaching of the scribes that Elijah would come first was based on Malachi 4: 5–6. The question of the disciples and Jesus' answer read more intelligibly if the second part of 12 in Mark (*How is it written . . .*) is taken as part of the enquiry of the disciples, either after 10 or after 11. They remembered Jesus' teaching in Mark 8: 31, about the suffering of the Son of Man. But it was not 'written' (in the Old Testament) of the Son of Man, that he should suffer; hence they asked for further explanation. Jesus seems to have linked again the term Son of Man with the idea of the suffering Servant of God.

85. *The cure of an epileptic boy*
Matthew 17: 14–20 Mark 9: 14–29 Luke 9: 37–43a

The account in Mark, containing many vivid features, is considerably abbreviated in Matthew and Luke. The boy's trouble was epilepsy, which was taken to be due to demon-possession. A graphic description is given in 18 of Mark of an attack. The words *pineth away* are literally 'he becomes rigid'—frequent in epileptic fits.

The English version obscures the play on words in 22–24 of Mark. *Canst* and *are possible* represent forms of the same Greek verb, while *faithless* (19) and *believe* come from the same root. Jesus echoed the father's words, *If thou canst do anything* . . . (if it is possible . . .) by replying: 'If it is possible! All things are possible for him who has faith.' The father replies: 'I have faith. Help my lack of faith.'

Mark says Jesus stressed to the disciples the need for prayer (29). *And fasting* was added in later manuscripts by scribes. Matthew says, not very suitably, that they lacked faith (20), but it was the faith of the father which cured the boy, not of the disciples.

(*c*) Return to Galilee

86. *The second statement of the Passion*

Matthew 17: 22–23 Mark 9: 30–32 Luke 9: 43b–45

For the other occasions on which Jesus warned the disciples of the fate in store for him at Jerusalem, see Sections 83 and 97. Jesus was here travelling *incognito* (30 in Mark), so that he might not attract a crowd, as he wished to teach the disciples privately.

87. *Teaching on true greatness*

Matthew 18: 1–5 Mark 9: 33–37 Luke 9: 46–48

This is the last time that Capernaum is mentioned in Mark. The disciples were probably arguing about who was to be greatest in the coming Kingdom (as Matt. indeed says) in their question to Jesus. The lesson in Matthew (4) is more suitable to this occasion than that in Mark (37) (cf. Section 94, where a child is again made an object-lesson). In both narratives Mark uses a Greek term, when speaking of Jesus' action, which suggests 'he took them in the crook of his arm'—omitted by Matthew and Luke.

88. *The coin in the fish's mouth*
Matthew 17: 24–27

The coin here called *the half-shekel* was a *didrachmon*, which every male Jew was supposed to give towards the maintenance of the Temple services. Two *didrachma* amounted to one *stater* (27). This would be hence the amount to be paid by two people.

Jesus' reply in 25–26 means: 'Earthly kings do not tax their own families (*toll* or *tribute* means customs taxes or capitation taxes), so God does not really demand payment from his sons.' This means those who share his character, as Jesus and the disciples were seeking to do. But for the sake of expediency (27; literally, 'that we may not scandalize them') Jesus was willing to pay the tax. . . . It is not said that Peter went and caught a fish and actually found a stater in its mouth. This is not a miracle-story. T. R. Glover suggests that this was Jesus' playful way of suggesting that Peter might do some work—go and catch some fish and so earn the money to pay the tax.

After the destruction of Jerusalem by the Romans in A.D. 70, they demanded that the payment of this tax should be continued but should go towards the upkeep of the temple of Jupiter. Christians were puzzled whether they ought to pay this tax or not and this paragraph was probably preserved and included here in order to help them. The contrast in 25–26 between *sons* and *strangers* is that between Christians and Jews (or Romans). For the sake of peace, the Christians are advised to continue payment of this (and presumably other) taxes to the Roman authorities (cf. Section 140).

89. *A lesson on tolerance*

Mark 9: 38–40 Luke 9: 49–50

This is the only time in the Synoptic Gospels that John speaks by himself. Generally he is associated with his brother James. His remark here is in accordance with the nickname of the two brothers—*sons of thunder* (cf. Section 99).

The man whom he wished to stop was exorcising or *driving out demons* in the name of Jesus (cf. the incident in Acts 19: 13). A formula when commanding demons to leave a sufferer was 'In the name of . . .', the exorcist using the name or authority of someone greater or of more powerful reputation than himself.' . . . The last sentence has its complement in Matthew 12: 30 and Luke 11: 23 (from Q): 'he who is not with me is against me'. There it is an appeal to an individual who might be neutral; here it is a principle laid down for Jesus' followers, in dealing with other people whose position might be considered doubtful.

90. *Teaching on offences and allied topics*

Matthew 18: 6–14 Mark 9: 41–50 Luke 17: 1–2

The whole paragraph in Mark (38–50) is really one section, in which different sayings of Jesus on related topics are gathered together. The statements are linked together by 'key-words': *name* in 39 leads to 40 (see Revised Version margin for the literal rendering); *stumble* in 42 leads to 43; *fire* in 48 leads to 49; and *salt* in 49 leads to 50.

All of this, with the exception of the last two verses in Mark, is paralleled in Matthew, who has also used some of it in the Sermon on the Mount (5: 28–30). He has also reproduced 41 of Mark in the charge to the twelve disciples (Matt. 10: 42). Luke has a parallel only to 42 of Mark, and here it comes from Q.

The *millstone* is a large stone, used in a mill, driven by an ass. Criminals were punished in Galilee by hanging a great stone around their necks when they were flung into the sea. Jesus used the term metaphorically, of course. *Entering into life* (44 in Mark) is the same as *entering the Kingdom of God* (47), i.e. taking one's place in the coming Realm. The opposite of this is the *Gehenna of fire*, the lot of those outside the Kingdom. On this term, see Section 45.

Verses 49–50 in Mark seem to consist of isolated sayings of Jesus. The general meaning is that his disciples must be purified and so able to purify others. The fire of suffering and persecution will do this. The latter part of 50 appropriately closes the whole section, which began a dispute between the disciples (33).

Matthew follows with a further paragraph, including a parable about a lost sheep (10–14). There is a parallel to this in Luke 15, probably from another source (see Section 122). . . . The Jews believed that nations had guardian *angels* and the idea is here extended to individuals (10). It was originally a Persian idea, adopted by the Jews. It is generally taken here as referring to children but it might mean any believer in Christ or even any who are 'lost'.

91. *On the agreement of brethren*
Matthew 18: 15–20

This is part of one of the discourses of Jesus compiled by Matthew (Chapter 18). Its subject is the relations between the disciples. Verses 1–14 are taken from Mark (see Section 87).

Verse 17 is one of the two places in the Gospels where the word *church* appears (see also Matt. 16: 18). This paragraph seems to presuppose an organized Church and it is generally agreed that in its present form at least it reflects the experiences and practices of the first-century Christians, although genuine sayings of Jesus lie behind it. There is a parallel to 15 in Luke 17:3 (next section), which is perhaps nearer the original word of Jesus.

The reference in 17 to the *Gentile* and the *publican* seems to reflect the Jewish prejudices of the writer. *Binding* and *loosing* were technical terms for forbidding and permitting. What was promised to Peter at Caesarea Philippi (Matt. 16: 19) is here given to the whole company of the disciples. Verse 20 explains 19. The mere fact that two or three people have decided on anything does not force God to endorse their decision as 19 might seem at first to imply. Jesus assumes that they have met and carefully considered the matter, with him among them (20) and so their decision is really his.

92. *On forgiveness. The parable of the unmerciful servant*
Matthew 18: 21–35 Luke 17: 3–4

The point of Jesus' reply to Peter in Matthew is that seven was the perfect number and the Jewish Rabbis reckoned that forgiveness of an offender for *seven times* was surely sufficient. Jesus said that forgiveness must be unlimited. It is not certain whether the number indicated here is seventy-seven or seventy times seven, i.e. 490. In either case, it is an emphatic hyperbole; the man would have lost count by that time!

The servant owed his master three million pounds and his fellow servant owed him twenty pounds (so Moffatt translates). . . . The lord was perfectly within his rights in demanding the sale of the man's household and his family (25). The *tormentors* were probably actual torturers, who were employed in the time of the Herods (34). The application is pointed in 35; it is similar to the comment added to the Lord's Prayer in Matthew 6: 15. The significant words seem to be *from your hearts*. It was the heart of the servant which was wrong and that was why he could not receive the forgiveness of his master.

IV. THE JOURNEY TO JERUSALEM

(*a*) The Account in Mark

93. *Judea: the question of divorce*

Matthew 19: 1–12 Mark 10: 1–12 Luke 16: 18

There is a definite change of scene in Mark 10: 1. This chapter is concerned with a journey to Jerusalem. There is a further indication of the progress of the journey in 32. By 46 the company have arrived at Jericho and at the beginning of chapter 11 they are in Jerusalem.

The Pharisees tried to trap Jesus here into giving his opinion. The question of the conditions of divorce was debated in the Rabbinic schools of the time. Jesus was probably asked to decide between two rival opinions. The followers of Rabbi Hillel allowed divorce *for any cause*, some of them for the most trifling reasons. The school of Shammai, a rival Rabbi, permitted divorce only for adultery. In his reply Jesus made a decision even more strict than that of the most severe Jews. Further, his saying put man and wife on a footing of equality, whereas in Jewish law an offence could be committed only by the wife against her husband and only the man could divorce the woman. Jesus also goes back to the original institution of marriage, according to the Old Testament account, to show that it was to be a true union. He was not legislating for future generations. What he was really forbidding or deprecating was a second marriage, after divocre. The stress is on the words *and marries again* (11–12 in Mark, 9 in Matt.).

There are parallels in Matthew 5: 31–32 (Section 46)—part of the Sermon on the Mount. This, like Luke 16: 18, comes from Q. Verses 11–12 in Matthew seem to be added from another context. They refer to self-denial for the sake of the Kingdom of God.

94. *The reception of childern*
Matthew 19: 13–15 Mark 10: 13–16 Luke 18: 15–17

In this context—the journey to Jerusalem—the children may have been brought to Jesus to say farewell. This might account for the churlish attitude of the disciples. The word used in Mark suggests very small children. The phrase *of such is the Kingdom of God* probably means: 'The Kingdom of God belongs to such', i.e. it is a gift to be received by those who would become like children. Similarly to *receive the Kingdom as a child* means to accept it as a gift in a childlike spirit. The Rabbis spoke of 'taking on oneself the Kingdom' by scrupulous observance of the Law. Jesus said it was to be accepted as a gift.

Cf. Section 87, where Jesus receives children to show where true greatness lies.

95. *The rich man*
Matthew 19: 16–30 Mark 10: 17–31 Luke 18: 18–30

The man is usually called the 'rich young ruler' —a combination of terms applied to him in the three accounts. Mark suggests perhaps middle-age, by the man's statement that he had observed the Law *from his youth.* Matthew calls him a young man and Luke says he was a ruler.

The man's greeting to Jesus, *Good master* (literally Rabbi), in Mark, was a piece of conventional flattery, which Jesus rejected. Matthew objected to Jesus' question, *Why callest thou me good?* and changed it (17). *Eternal life*, about which the man asked, is a synonym for the Kingdom of God. Only Mark records that Jesus *loved him* (21). The final reply of Jesus shows that the man's riches were hindering him from really fulfilling the Law.

The sequel, after the departure of the rich man, is a talk by Jesus to the disciples about wealth in the Kingdom. The phrase about *a camel* going through *the eye of a needle* was probably a proverbial expression. There was a similar Babylonian saying about an elephant. It means a feat of extreme difficulty or an impossibility. There is no foundation for the idea that *eye of a needle* meant a small gate in a city wall. The suggestion probably arose from literal-minded people who could not see that Jesus was deliberately using an exaggeration, in Eastern fashion.

Jesus' promises to those who forsook all to follow him are not of course to be taken literally; but it is true that Christians who have left all have found abundant recompense.

Matthew adds 28 (cf. Luke 22: 30). *The regeneration* was a phrase used by the Greek Stoics and also by the apocalyptic writers. It meant the world transformed and reborn, at the coming of the new era or the Kingdom of God. *Judging the twelve tribes* means governing Israel, which is here presumably another name for the Kingdom of God. Jesus was making use of current imagery in order to impress on his followers the recompense they would receive for having left all for his sake.

96. *The parable of the labourers in the vineyard*
Matthew 20: 1–16

Matthew adds this as a further illustration of Jesus' teaching about social relations, after his talk about wealth in the Kingdom. The point of the parable is that need, not desert, is what is taken into consideration when a man is called to the Kingdom of God. The climax of the story is in 15. Moffatt's translation well brings out the master's remark: 'Have you a grudge because I am generous?' Jesus means that in his relations with men God is generous, not a strict employer who gives men simply their deserts.

The *penny* was the *denarius*, the usual day's wage. The phrase in 4—*whatsoever is right I will give thee*—means the right proportion of the daily payment which was due.

97. *The third statement of the Passion*
Matthew 20: 17–19 Mark 10: 32–34 Luke 18: 31–34

The previous predictions of Jesus' fate at Jerusalem are in Sections 83 and 86. This is the most detailed of them all. This is also the first time in which Jerusalem is definitely mentioned as the goal of the journey in Mark 10.

Verse 32 in Mark in a graphic picture. T. R. Glover comments: 'He is moving to Jerusalem with a purpose . . . wrapped in thought. His pace quickens and they find themselves at a distance behind him. . . . As they follow the wonder deepens into fear' (see *The Jesus of History*).

98. *The request of James and John*
Matthew 20: 20–28 Mark 10: 35–45

The story in Mark is true to the character of the two brothers, as 'sons of thunder'. Matthew wished to spare the two apostles, who were revered figures, so he introduced their mother and in his account she makes the request on behalf of her sons. Even in Matthew, however, the mother drops out after 21. The account in Mark is more natural and realistic.

The request shows that the disciples were still looking for the glorious and visible Kingdom of the Messiah. They ignored or still misunderstood Jesus' teaching about the necessity for service and humility. *Right* and *left* are the places of honour by the side of a monarch as he sits on his throne. . . . In his reply Jesus used metaphors familiar from the Old Testament—*cup* and *baptism* both mean suffering. James was indeed murdered by Herod Agrippa I (Acts 12: 2); there is an uncertain tradition that John also was martyred early in the Church's history.

The story concludes with Jesus' teaching to the other ten disciples. There is a parallel to this in Luke 22: 24–27, delivered at the Last Supper. *The rulers* referred to are the Roman and other Gentile rulers. Their attitude towards their subjects is well expressed in the phrase *they lord it over them*. *Their great ones* are the subordinate officials. The Greek word translated *minister* should really be 'servant' and that translated *servant* should be 'slave'.

The last verse uses a metaphor to describe the service of the Son of Man (some think this verse was added to Jesus' words, as a comment by a Christian preacher or writer). The word *ransom* generally meant in the Old Testament a compensation paid for a life or for the liberation of slaves or captives. The Jews also thought of God's deliverance of their nation from slavery in Egypt, in this way. In the New Testament world the Greek word was used to denote a deliverance, especially a costly one. The metaphor of a ransom here must not be pressed; there is no suggestion of a payment being made to anyone. The thought behind the statement is probably that of the Servant Songs of Deutero-Isaiah, especially Isaiah 53: 11–12, where the word *many* is used in a somewhat similar manner. There are other places also in the Gospels where the term Son of Man is linked with the idea of the Suffering Servant.

(*b*) Luke's Travel-narrative

99. *The beginning of the journey. The Samaritan village*
Luke 9: 51–56

Sections 93–98 have dealt with the account of the journey to Jerusalem given in Mark 10. This narrative is followed by Matthew. In Section 131 the company arrive at Jericho. Luke, however, devotes nine chapters to this journey (9: 51–18: 14) and introduces a large amount of material, both incidents and teaching, between the departure from Galilee and the arrival at Jericho. (Whether all this took place on this journey is doubtful.) Luke has matter here from Q and his own special L. There are consequently some parallels in Matthew in these sections (99–130).

The phrase in 51—*that he should be received up*—translates one term—'his assumption'. Luke is thinking of the stages by which Jesus reached his ascended glory. Possibly the reference is to the actual journey to the capital—*up* to Jerusalem. . . . Jesus sought a lodging in a Samaritan village but the villagers exhibited the usual attitude of their race towards Jews—an attitude returned by the disciples. James and John act up to their nickname. For other Lukan references to Samaritans see 10: 33 and 17: 16.

100. *Various would-be followers*

Matthew 8: 18–22 Luke 9: 57–62

The setting in Luke seems to explain better the sternness of Jesus than the context in Matthew. It was at the beginning of the journey to Jerusalem and Jesus emphasized that it was now or never for those who would follow him.

In Jesus, reply to the first man, the term Son of Man is used in striking contrast to the popular picture of the Son of Man who would come in glory. . . . It is not said that the father of the second man was already dead. Probably he meant: 'Let me wait a little longer, until I am relieved of the responsibility of lóoking after my father'. . . . For the third man (in Luke only) to bid farewell to his friends and relatives would be, in the East, a long ceremonial business. By the time these men had completed these duties, it would be too late for them to follow Jesus.

101. *The mission of the seventy disciples*

Matthew 9: 35–38, Luke 10: 1–20
11: 20–24

The parallel in Matthew 9 is Jesus' saying about the need for workers, while Matthew 11 contains the doom pronounced on the Galilaean towns which rejected Jesus' message works.

Only Luke records the sending out of seventy disciples. (Some ancient manuscripts read seventy-two here.) Seventy (or seventy-two) was supposed to be the number of nations in the world. As the twelve disciples represented the mission to Israel, so Luke thought of these as the Gentile mission. Some students think that this account of Jesus' instructions to them is but another version of his charge to the twelve, taken by Luke from Q. In Matthew 10 (Section 71) there is combined the account in Mark 6: 7ff with the Q account given here separately by Luke.

J. W. Bowman has recently made this suggestion: numbers were indicated in Greek manuscripts by letters and there is only a slight difference between twelve and seventy-two as indicated thus. Twelve may have been the original reading here, which became changed to seventy-two by a slip of a scribe copying the manuscript.

The usual Eastern salutation on entering a house—'Peace to you'—is referred to in 5–6. *The labourer is worthy of his hire* (7; *his food* in Matt. 10: 10) is a saying of Jesus which is apparently referred to in 1 Corinthians 9: 7, 14 and in 1 Timothy 5: 18. The phrase *The Kingdom of God is come* (or, *has come*) *upon you* (9) is another instance of Jesus' teaching about the Kingdom of God as already present (cf. Luke 17: 20–21). *Sodom* (12) is referred to as a city of wickedness and one which insulted its visitors.

In the doom on the Galilaean towns, Chorazin was a town two miles north of Capernaum. Bethsaida was just north of the Lake of Galilee. Tyre and Sidon are taken as typical heathen and foreign cities.

Only Luke gives any detailed account of what Jesus said on the return of the disciples from their tour (17–20). *Satan fallen as lightning* is generally taken to mean that Jesus had a vision of the downfall of evil. It is, however, possible to regard the figure of lightning as representing blasting, destructive power. The battle against the Kingdom of God had begun. The promise to *tread on snakes* in 19 was probably meant symbolically of triumph over evil.

102. *The exultation of Jesus*

Matthew 11: 25–30, 13: 16–17 — Luke 10: 21–24

In Luke this is part of Jesus' response to the return of the disciples from their tour. The first verses (21–22 in Luke; 25–27 in Matt. 11) are common to both Gospels.

The *all things* which Jesus claims may mean 'all authority and power'; or perhaps the phrase means 'All my teaching has a divine authority'. Luke adds a blessing on the disciples because of the things which they see and hear (found also in Matt. 13, in the discussion about parables). *The things* referred to may mean the coming of the Kingdom of God among men, as proclaimed by Jesus.

Matthew adds the invitation of Jesus to those who *labour and are heavy laden* (11: 28–30). The heavy laden may be those burdened by the weight of the Jewish Law. 'The yoke of the Law' was a common expression in Jewish writings, and Jesus may have used *my yoke* by way of contrast. *I will give you rest* is well translated by Moffatt, 'I will refresh you', bringing out the purpose of such rest. *For I am meek* could be translated 'Learn of me, that I am meek. . . .'

103. *The parable of the good Samaritan*

Luke 10: 25–37

The introduction to the parable is reminiscent of the situation in Section 142. There, however, the questioner was a scribe who asked Jesus about the Law and Jesus himself quoted the two Old Testament commandments.

The parable does not strictly answer the question *Who is my neighbour?* It gives instead an example of true neighbourliness. The story is not to be taken as an allegory. . . . This is the only mention in Jesus' teaching of priests or Levites (31–32). The latter were subsidiary priests at the Temple at Jerusalem. The *two pence* were *denarii*. The man sacrificed two days' wages. The lawyer would not name the Samaritan (37), but paraphrased, to avoid admitting that the hated Samaritan was a better neighbour than the Jews who passed by.

104. *Martha and Mary*

Luke 10: 38–42

The *certain village* where Martha and Mary lived is not named. It does not seem to be Bethany, for this incident is on the road to Jerusalem and Bethany is not named until Luke 19: 28.

The phrase *cumbered* in 40 is literally 'torn in different directions', i.e. distracted. . . . The Greek text in 42 is uncertain. It may be *One thing is necessary* or *Few things are necessary*, or *Few things are necessary, or one.* Some people think it referred originally to the dishes: 'Do not prepare an elaborate meal.' There is probably a double meaning. Moffatt brings this out in the latter part of the verse: 'Mary has chosen the best dish and she is not to be dragged away from it.' Perhaps the *one thing necessary* which Mary had chosen was sincerity. Martha would really have liked to have sat with Mary and listened to Jesus but she was determined to attend to what she considered her 'duty'. Mary, more honest and genuine, let the meal go. Jesus always valued sincerity.

105. *The parable of the friend at midnight*

Luke 11: 5–8

In Luke this follows the Lord's Prayer (Section 50) and is followed by sayings of Jesus about prayer (Section 56).

The details of an Eastern home are vividly portrayed here—the man assuming his neighbour would give him some bread (three small Jewish loaves); the family all asleep, on the floor, so that the father would have to disturb them all to get to the door! . . . The point of the parable is an *a fortiori* argument, as in Luke 11: 13. The parable of the unrighteous judge, also found only in Luke, is similar (Section 129).

106. *The unclean spirit*

Matthew 12: 43–45 Luke 11: 24–26

In Luke this comes in the account of the accusation of Jesus' enemies that he was using the power of Beelzebub—Luke 11: 14–26 (see Section 28). Matthew, however, places these verses at the end of the story of the demand for a sign (Section 108).

The passage is a warning to those who have been freed from the power of evil. Something more powerful must be put in its place. The human spirit is compared to a house which has been spring-cleaned. Jesus was drawing a comparison between the state of mind of a demoniac and the Jewish people of his time. They might have been freed from pagan beliefs and practices and other evil things—but little of positive worth had been put in the place of these.

107. *The cry of the woman*

Luke 11: 27–28

With this short incident may be compared Jesus' sayings about his true relations (Section 29). Here also Jesus pointed out that spiritual affinity and the practice of God's will are more important than family ties.

A familiar Jewish salutation on meeting a friend was 'Blessed is thy mother'. Jesus did not want this conventional flattery.

108. *The demand for a sign*

Matthew 12: 38–42 Luke 11: 29–32

Mark also contains an account of the Pharisees asking for a sign (Section 81). By a *sign* Jesus' enemies probably meant something which would be indisputable evidence of his authority. Jesus in his reply called his contemporaries *an evil generation* (Luke) or *an adulterous generation* (Matt.) This would mean for his hearers a God-forsaking people. Adultery is a frequent synonym in the Old Testament for idolatry.

In Mark 8 Jesus refused to give any sign at all. Here the only sign is that of Jonah. Matthew explains this as referring to Jesus' own burial and resurrection. This seems a stretched analogy, and in actual fact Jesus was not *three days and three nights in the heart of the earth*; further, his resurrection was not a sign or proof to his enemies, for they did not witness it. Most critics today consider that 40 in Matthew represents the interpretation of Jesus' words which was current later in the Church, when Matthew wrote. *The sign of Jonah* probably referred to the prophet's preaching. According to the Old Testament book, he was sent to proclaim judgment to the people of Nineveh (see 32 in Luke). So Jesus was a messenger of God to the people of his generation and the only 'sign' they should require was his preaching, if they responded to that.

The queen of the south was the queen of Sheba, who came to Jerusalem to visit Solomon (1 Kings 10). Heathen people like her and the inhabitants of Nineveh would be judged more worthy than the Jews of Jesus' day. *A greater than Solomon* (or Jonah) is literally 'something greater'. This may refer to the Kingdom of God, which had already come, in Jesus' work.

109. *Warnings against the Pharisees*

Matthew 23: 1–36 Luke 11: 37–54

Luke introduces this section of Jesus' teaching by relating it to a meal to which he was invited by a Pharisee. This setting was probably provided by Luke himself, for we cannot imagine Jesus abusing the hospitality of his host by taking the opportunity to denounce him and his associates. In Matthew the passage from Q (which Luke reproduces) has been joined with other matter, to form one of the long discourses of Jesus. The setting in Matthew is in Jerusalem.

Luke's account:

The complaint that Jesus had not washed before dinner (37) is reminiscent of the complaint about his disciples (Mark 7: 1ff). It refers to the ritual washings of the Pharisees, not to simple cleanliness. . . . Verse 41 is obscure. It is possible that the phrase translated *give alms* represents an Aramaic expression which should be rendered *purify* (cf. 26 in Matt.). Verse 42 (23 in Matt.) refers to the Old Testament law which laid down that *the fruit of the land*—corn, oil and wine—had to be tithed, i.e. a tenth part had to be devoted to God. The scribes in their tradition extended this to all herbs.

Verse 44 refers to hidden burying places. Those who walked above them did not suspect that the tombs were beneath them. To touch a grave was to render oneself unclean. So the Pharisees are declared to be a real source of danger to the people, because their evil is unsuspected. Verses 47–48 (29–31 in Matt.) mean that the Jews reverenced only dead saints and prophets, but if the heroes of the past (whom their forefathers killed but whose memory they pretended to honour) could live they would treat them in the same way as their fathers had done. Verses 49–51 (34–36 in Matt.) are a quotation in Luke from *the wisdom of God*. Some think Jesus was quoting from an apocryphal book, but none with such a title has been found. More probably the phrase meant 'God in his wisdom', and it may be a summary of the message of the Old Testament. The murder of Abel (Gen. 4) is the first recorded in Old Testament history while Zachariah's death was the last (2 Chron. 24: 22; this was the last book as arranged in the Hebrew Bible). The reference in Matthew to *the son of Barachiah* is probably a mistake.

Matthew's account:

The tone here seems very bitter and it is generally agreed that the writer has exaggerated the faults of the Pharisees and the vehemence of Jesus' denunciation. He has put here e.g. (as part of Jesus' words) (33) a statement previously attributed to John the Baptist (Matt. 3: 7).

Verses 2–3 may mean simply 'on the whole' the teaching of the scribes and Pharisees, as the successors of Moses the lawgiver, had full authority as an interpretation of the Law. Or was Jesus being ironical? The *phylacteries* (5) were small leathern cases (the word means literally 'protecting charms' or 'amulets') which were worn—and still are—on the wrists and forehead by strict Jews when at prayer. They contained quotations from the Law, in literal obedience to the command in Deuteronomy 6: 8.

Matthew then arranges seven *woes* (13–32) (14 is omitted in the best authorities, as an insertion from Mark 12: 40). A *proselyte* (15) was originally a foreigner living in Palestine among the Jews, but the word was used later in a religious sense for one who adopted Judaism. Theoretically proselytes were reckoned as equals by the Jews, but in practice they were often regarded as inferiors.

Verses 16–22 are examples of Jewish casuistry—hair-splitting in the matter of religious oaths (cf. Matt. 5: 33–37). Verse 24 refers to the Pharisee's drinking. He was careful to *strain out* the small gnat from his wine, passing it through a muslin strainer. The humorous exaggeration is obvious. Verse 27 (cf. 44 in Luke) refers to tombs which have been whitened on the outside to warn passers-by of their presence. They look very clean outside, but inside they are full of decaying bodies. So were the hearts and real purposes of the Pharisees.

110. *Instruction and encouragement for the disciples*

Luke 12: 1–12

Almost all this section is paralleled in Matthew in different contexts—1 is in Matthew 16: 5–6 (and Mark 8: 14–15), 2–9 are in Matthew 10: 26–33, as part of the charge to the twelve disciples, 10 is in Matthew 12: 31–32 (and Mark 3: 28–29) and 11–12 are in Matthew 10: 19–20. Most of the points to be noted in the version in Luke have been dealt with in Sections 71 and 28.

Leaven is a metaphor (1) for influence, generally in the New Testament with a bad meaning. The phrase in 2 means, the things and sayings (of the Pharisees) which are hypocritically hidden will come to light. In Matthew 10: 26–27 this saying is an instruction to the disciples to proclaim in public what Jesus had told them in private.

111. *The parable of the rich foolish man*

Luke 12: 13–21

Like some other Lukan parables, this is rather an illustrative story than a true parable or comparison. Its occasion was the demand to Jesus to legislate in a family dispute. The Jews used to appeal to the Rabbis for decisions regarding the application of the Old Testament laws of inheritance.

Jesus' answer (15) may be taken as applying to two classes of people. To the poor he says *Beware of covetousness*, and to the rich 'Your possessions are not your real life'. . . . The Revised Version in 20, *thou foolish one*, is an improvement on 'Thou fool'. The Greek word is not the same as that which Jesus forbade his followers to use in Matthew 5: 22.

Luke follows this story with a passage of teaching (22–34) consisting of warning about being anxious in worldly matters and speaking of the true treasure (see Sections 54 and 52).

112. *The need for watchfulness*

Matthew 24: 42–51 Luke 12: 35–48

In Matthew this is part of the apocalyptic discourse (after Section 149). There is no parallel in Matthew to 35–38 in Luke.

The opening in Luke speaks of Eastern marriage customs. The Syrian bridegroom goes to bring his bride to his home and his servants remain behind to get the house ready for him. . . . Verse 37 in Luke expresses unusual behaviour on the part of a master, but emphasizes the lesson of humility. The three watches (38) represent the Jewish way of measuring the night. The Romans reckoned four watches.

Jesus then speaks of the coming of the Son of Man (40 in Luke, 44 in Matt.). The past tense in the previous verse—*if the master had known*—suggests that originally Jesus referred to the Jews of his day; the Son of Man had come, like an unexpected thief, and the people were not ready for him. The same lesson on the need for watchfulness is enforced in the parable of the good and bad servants (42–48 in Luke, 45–51 in Matt.).

A number of sayings and parables seem to have been collected here. Their general purpose was to warn the disciples that they must be on the look-out for some great crisis. Jesus may have been referring to the trial to come on the disciples when his enemies got their way in Jerusalem; or he may have meant the crisis coming upon the Jews when the Romans decided to put down their attempts at revolt.

113. *The fire and the sword of Jesus*
Matthew 10: 34–36 Luke 12: 49–53

This passage has been partly used by Matthew in the charge to the twelve disciples (Section 71).

The opening verse should probably be translated: 'How earnestly I wish it were kindled!' Jesus longed to fulfil the words of John the Baptist, about one who would baptize with fire. Baptism is also used as a metaphor for suffering (cf. Mark 10: 38). Jesus then warns the disciples of the results of his coming. It does not of course mean that this was the *purpose* of his coming.

114. *The significance of the heavens*
Matthew 16: 2–3 Luke 12: 54–59

In Matthew this is part of Jesus' answer to those who demanded a sign (see Section 81); but verses 2–3 were probably not in the Gospel as originally written, as the best manuscripts omit them.

In Luke the reference is to the wind. If it was in the west, it meant rain from the Mediterranean. If it was from the south, it was the hot wind from the desert. This may be a general warning to the disciples to be ready for an impending crisis, as in Luke 12: 35–38 (Section 112). It is, however, possible that it should be linked with 13: 1–9 (next section)—a warning to the Jews of Jesus' own day about the consequences of their course of action. The passage is followed in Luke by the saying about settling with one's adversary (57–59; for notes on this see Section 45). Jesus advised the Jews to come to terms with the Romans (58) before it was too late, instead of continuing to plot against him. *This time* (56) means the crisis in which the nation found itself. We may compare the teaching of Jeremiah, when Jerusalem was threatened by the Babylonians.

115. *The need for repentance. The parable of the fig-tree*

Luke 13: 1–9

These two paragraphs both contain a warning to the Jewish nation of Jesus' day. Verses 1–5 tell of the results of their continued opposition to the Romans. This is what they were to repent of. *The Galilaeans* were probably in revolt against the Romans; Galilee was always a hotbed of disturbance and nationalistic feeling. The *eighteen men* on whom the tower fell may have been undermining it. Nothing else is known of these incidents but Josephus mentions an attack by Pilate's soldiers on a riotous assembly of the Jews. Jesus said that all the nation would perish similarly, unless they changed their ways—a forecast which was fulfilled in the events of A.D. 70.

Verses 6–9 have the same theme. The symbolism of the vineyard and the fig-tree was common in the Old Testament to represent the nation of Israel. Jesus said that Judaism had one more chance to change its ways.

116. *The healing of an infirm woman*

Luke 13: 10–17

The phrase used in 11 is literally 'a woman who had a spirit of weakness'. Perhaps her trouble was nervous prostration. This is another Sabbath controversy about healing (cf. Sections 25 and 118).

Jesus' reply to the complaint of the synagogue ruler or elder referred to acts of kindliness on the Sabbath, which the Law in general allowed. There is a play upon words here, in the comparison between *loosing cattle* from their stall and *loosing* or freeing the woman from her infirmity.

Luke follows this with parables of the Kingdom of God (13: 18–21) (the mustard seed and the leaven) and other sayings (13: 22–30) (the narrow way, the confession of lordship, strangers in the Kingdom of God). See Sections 35, 37, 58, 60, 61.

117. *Herod and Jesus. The lament over Jerusalem*

Matthew 23: 37–39 Luke 13: 31–35

Verses 31–33 in Luke are not found elsewhere. Jesus was apparently still in the territory of Herod Antipas—either Galilee or Perea. . . . *Fox* (32) stand for us for cunning, but in the East it denotes destructiveness. There is also some evidence that among Jewish Rabbis the fox meant 'a worthless, insignificant man'. This would certainly apply to Herod. . . . *I am perfected* means 'I will finish my task'. Jesus' general meaning is: 'I am going to continue my work, in spite of Herod's threats.' *On the third day* was an expression meaning 'in a short time'. The reference to the deaths of prophets in Jerusalem (33) is grim irony.

In Luke this is followed immediately by the lament over Jerusalem. In Matthew the words are spoken in the city itself. The phrase *Your house is left* (*desolate*) probably means 'The Temple is abandoned' (i.e. by God) because of the unworthy character of the inhabitants of the city and the worshippers. The saying *Blessed is he that cometh* . . . is a quotation from Psalm 118: 26. This was used to welcome pilgrims to the Jewish feasts at the Temple. Luke intends this to refer to Jesus' entry into Jerusalem, which is still to come. In Matthew, however, this event is past, so he may be thinking of a future 'coming' of Jesus.

118. *The healing of the man with dropsy*

Luke 14: 1–6

For other stories of healing on the Sabbath, see Sections 25 and 116. . . . Hospitality was indulged in on the Sabbath by Jews. There are other occasions in Luke where Jesus was invited by a Pharisee to a meal (7: 36 and 11: 37).

Jesus' question (3) is reminiscent of Mark 3: 4, while 5 is like his question in Luke 13: 15. Whether the Law allowed it or not, a Jew would rescue a stricken animal on the Sabbath—how much more a man; says Jesus.

119. *On humility and generosity at feasts*

Luke 14: 7–14

As on a previous occasion, the setting in Luke is probably not the correct one (see notes on Section 109). These remarks of Jesus may have been delivered on different occasions. . . . The sayings are a *parable* (7), i.e. they are not a list of rules for social behaviour but a description of the attitude of mind which Jesus' followers should always exhibit—humility and generosity. Jesus was also probably warning the Jews of his time against the loss of their national privileges. A familiar symbol of the Messianic age was that of a great banquet (see next section also). The Jews naturally expected to be entitled to the chief seats; instead, they ought to be humble.

The Eastern table was round or oval and the guests reclined on their left arm, eating with the right hand. The chief seat would not be at the 'head' of the table but in the centre of the settee. The next place of honour was on the left hand of the man in the centre and the next place was on his right.

120. *The parable of the feast*

Matthew 22: 1–14 Luke 14: 15–24

These two parables are a contrast as well as a parallel. Possibly one story of Jesus has come down in two different forms or they may represent quite distinct parables.

The parable of the great supper (Luke) is attached to the sayings in the previous section. In the East the host used to send a servant to repeat the invitation as the time for the meal drew near (17). To reply with an excuse after such a reminder would be a grave discourtesy. The shallowness of the excuses offered by the guests is obvious. . . . The *streets and lanes* (21) are the open places and the narrow streets of the city. *Constrain them* (23) probably means 'invite them again'. It is said to be polite behaviour in Syria to decline an invitation the first time it is offered.

The parable of the wedding feast (Matt.) has a different setting. The host is a king. The story seems, however, to have become mixed with another about some rebellious subjects of a monarch. Verses 6–7 were probably inserted here by the writer or an editor. Without these, 1–10 reads quite intelligibly and the parable is similar to that in Luke. . . . The *partings of the highways* (9) are the cross-roads, where the poor would be found begging.

The parable of the man without a wedding garment (11–14) is quite separate. The opening of this story was probably like 2. It is obviously out of place here, for people drawn from the streets would not be expected to have suitable clothes for a wedding. The parable reflects the Jewish practice by which the guests at a marriage, after the ceremony, proceeded to the feast, wearing their wedding clothes.

All three parables have much the same point. In the great supper and the wedding feast the banquet is the Kingdom of God. The Jews had been invited (by God) but they had made excuses, neglecting their spiritual duties and so proving themselves unworthy. So the outcasts and outsiders were invited instead. Jesus meant probably sinners, such as he associated with, and Gentiles. In the parable of the wedding-garment, there is the same warning. Those who were invited to the feast did not come prepared, so they were cast outside.

121. *On taking up one's cross and counting the cost*

Luke 14: 25–35

Matthew has given the first part in the instructions to the twelve disciples (Matt. 10: 37–39). In Luke Jesus is on the way to Jerusalem and warns people of the conditions under which they must follow him.

The term *hate* (26) (Matt. tones it down) means in the eastern idiom 'love less'. Jesus used a grim metaphor when speaking of *taking up a cross*. The only man in the Roman world who had to do this was on his way to execution!

The parables in 28–33 are found only in Luke. They have in common the idea of counting the cost before embarking on any enterprise. Jesus demanded such an attitude for his followers. . . . The *tower* (28) may be a watch-tower for a vineyard, where the owner looked out for robbers.

Luke follows this with teaching about the influence of salt (14: 34–35) (see Section 43).

122. *Three parables of the lost*

Luke 15: 1–32

In Luke these parables were given in defence of Jesus' action in welcoming sinners and tax-collectors.

The lost sheep has a parallel in Matthew 18: 10–14, probably from a different source (Section 90). The care of the Eastern shepherd over his flock is reflected in 3–7. He goes before them and knows each one individually.

The lost coin (8–10) may be a reminiscence of Jesus' own home-life, when Mary lost some money. The piece of silver was a *drachma*, a Greek silver coin which was practically the equivalent of a Roman denarius. It would be a considerable loss to a poor housewife.

The prodigal son (11–32) has been called the perfect short story—in any translation. . . . *Thy substance* (12) means the father's estate. By Jewish law he could thus dispose of his property and the younger son was entitled to one-third (Deut. 1: 17). The meaning of *gathered all together* is 'he realized his share', i.e. converted it into ready money. For a Jew to *feed swine* (16) would be the lowest degradation. The *husks* would be the pods of the carob tree, which were used as fodder for animals and as food for the very poor.

The latter part of the son's intended speech is cut short by the father (cf. 19 and 21). *The best robe* is literally 'the first robe', one especially kept for ceremonial occasions. Only the lowest people, such as slaves, went without *ring* or *sandals*. The elder brother is evidently intended to represent the Pharisees. The story finishes where it should, to leave its own impression on the hearer. Any moralizing addition or sequel would spoil it.

123. *The parable of the dishonest steward*

Luke 16: 1–13

Many interpretations have been proposed both of this difficult parable and of the teaching which follows. There seem to be four separate sections here:

(i) The parable itself (1–7) is about a landowner and his bailiff. The steward seems to hold the I.O.U.s of his master's debtors. Perhaps they were debts incurred in receiving produce from the estate. He hands the slips back and invites the debtors to change the figures to lower amounts—obviously a dishonest proceeding. The *measure* in 6 is a liquid measure, about eight and three-quarter gallons. The *measure* in 7 is about seven bushels.

Verse 8 seems to be a comment on this parable. It seems extraordinary that the master should praise his dishonest steward (8a). There is, however, no word for 'his' before *lord* in the Greek—it is *the lord*—and this may be the comment of the writer or a preacher saying that Jesus commended the steward—not for his morality but for his astuteness. The latter part of the verse reinforces this. The disciples of Jesus (*the sons of light*) should exercise as much keenness and acumen in their affairs. *The sons of this world* (or, rather, *age*) are those who are concerned with their own generation, i.e. the affairs of this time.

(ii) Verse 9 may be an application of the parable but is probably a saying taken from another occasion—general advice to make good use of material things. Possibly Jesus was being sarcastic. The suggestion has, however, been made that *by means of* (literally 'out of') has really the meaning of 'apart from'. The teaching then is: Make friends quite apart from considerations of material wealth, which is bound to fail. Then your true friends will still be with you. *The mammon of unrighteousness* is a phrase meaning the mammon (or wealth) which produces so much unrighteousness.

(iii) Verses 10–12 are also sayings from another occasion and teach a quite different lesson—the necessity for faithfulness, both in material and spiritual matters.

(iv) Verse 13 is another separate saying, calling men to choose between slavery to material wealth and service to God. It is paralleled in Matthew 6: 24 (see Section 53).

124. *The self-righteousness of the Pharisees. The validity of the Jewish Law*

Luke 16: 14–18

Verses 14–15 have no parallel elsewhere. The phrase *they scoffed at him* (14) is literally 'they held up their noses in scorn at him'. The same term is used in Luke 23: 35. The Pharisees *justified themselves before men* (15) presumably by giving alms, etc., in public (cf. Matt. 6, 2). They showed themselves to be righteous, i.e. 'self-righteous'. (cf. Section 130).

Verses 16–17 in Luke are paralleled in Matthew 5: 18

and 11, 12–13 (see Sections 44 and 73). Verse 18 is the only reference in Luke to Jesus' teaching about divorce. Fuller teaching is given in Matthew 5: 31–32 and Mark 10: 1–12 (Matt. 19: 1–12) (see Sections 46 and 93).

125. *The parable of the rich man and Lazarus*

Luke 16: 19–31

The point of this story is the responsibility of wealth and the hardening effect on men of riches. There are two themes: (i) that those who are afflicted in this life receive compensation in the next, while those who have plenty here suffer deprivation in the next; (ii) that the return of one from the dead would not convince those who have disregarded Moses and the prophets, i.e. the Old Testament teaching.

The details given of the after-life should not be pressed. Jesus was making use of current Jewish ideas and terms—Abraham's bosom, Hades, the flame of fire, a great gulf. Perhaps he was using or modifying a popular story already known to his hearers.

This is the only parable where a person has a name (20). Lazarus was a common Jewish name, meaning 'helped by God'. The rich man is often called Dives—the Latin for 'rich'. The action of the dogs in licking the sores of the beggar (21) was probably not meant for kindness but was an aggravation of his terrible condition. Dogs in the East are unclean animals.

Abraham's bosom is probably a reference to the idea of the state of the blessed after death as partaking of a banquet. The man on the right side of the host was able, as he reclined, to lean back on his bosom. *Hades* was the Greek name for the Hebrew *sheol*, the shadowy place for the departed in the Old Testament. Here it seems to have the character of Gehenna or Hell. The usual Hebrew idea was that all the departed spirits waited in Sheol, but here men are thought of as going straight to Paradise or to Gehenna. *Paradise* is from a Persian word meaning a park and was used for a place of pleasantness or blessedness (cf. Luke 23: 43).

126. *On faith and on service*

Luke 17: 5–10

Luke 17: 1–10 is a collection of sayings of Jesus on various topics. Verses 1–2 (on offences) and 3–4 (on forgiveness) are paralleled in Mark and Matthew (see Sections 90 and 92). The saying on the power of faith (5–6) is attached by Matthew to the story of the epileptic boy (Matt. 17: 20). Matthew has, however, *this mountain* for *this sycamine tree*—probably the black mulberry tree. A similar saying is found in Mark 11: 23 (Matt. 21: 21). In each case a proverbial saying is used, with typical eastern hyperbole. The phrase about uprooting or removing mountains is mentioned by Paul in 1 Corinthians 13: 2.

A parable about service follows (7–10), the general meaning of which is that there is no merit in serving God. Jesus borrows a metaphor from slavery. The word translated *unprofitable* (10) may represent a popular formula about servants—'good-for-nothing slaves'.

127. *The healing of ten lepers*

Luke 17: 11–19

The situation is still the journey to Jerusalem (11). Samaria was entered in Luke 9: 52.

As in a previous story (Section 20), Jesus told the lepers to show themselves to the priest in accordance with the Jewish Law. The point of the incident is that the only one who gave thanks was a despised Samaritan. The others were presumably Jews, although this is not stated. *This stranger* (18) is literally 'this alien'—spoken from the standpoint of the Jews.

128. *The coming of the Kingdom of God and the day of the Son of Man*

Matthew 24: 26–28, 37–41 — Luke 17: 20–37

Verses 20–21 in Luke are not found elsewhere. The current expectation was that the Kingdom came *with observation* (Moffatt: 'as you hope to catch sight of it'). Apocalyptic writers depicted the 'signs' which would precede its arrival. Jesus swept aside, as here, all such excited expectations. . . . The last words of 21 may be translated: (i) *within you.* This means that the Kingdom is not something established externally but is to be found within human hearts and lives. Jesus was stressing the inward nature of the Kingdom. Some think, however, that this is unlikely, since he was addressing Pharisees. (ii) *in your midst.* This accords with other teaching of Jesus about the Kingdom of God as already at hand or as present (cf. Mark 1: 15; Luke 11: 20).

A long section follows in Luke (22–37) about the *day of the Son of Man.* It is paralleled in Matthew 24, where this matter (from Q) is joined with the material in Mark. 13 (Sections 145–149). *One of the days of the Son of Man* (22 in Luke) probably means one of the days of the new age which the Messiah was expected to inaugurate. Matthew (26) is more definite. The expected Messiah is here rumoured to be some revolutionary leader in the desert or among the tombs —giving strange teaching in a strange place. The comparison with lightning (24 in Luke, 27 in Matt.) is in the suddennesss of its appearance and also perhaps in the fact that it can be seen over a wide area.

In the second part (26–37 in Luke, 37–41 in Matt.) people are warned by the destruction which fell upon the contemporaries of Noah and Lot, because they were not prepared. Then the paragraph seems to turn to the confusion caused by the sudden invasion of an enemy army (31 and 34–37 in Luke). There would be no time for a man to go home to fetch his goods and people would be taken indiscriminately. This suits the circumstances of the Roman attack on Judea in A.D. 68. The final comment (37 in Luke) is given earlier in Matthew (28). The word *eagles* is literally 'vultures'. It sounds like a popular proverb. One can tell the presence of a carcase in the desert by the birds of prey hovering around. Perhaps Jesus meant that Judaism was a rotting corpse; its doom was near.

129. *The parable of the unrighteous judge*

Luke 18: 1–8

This is another of Luke's special parables about prayer (cf. Sections 105 and 130).

Justice in the East has not always been known for its impartiality! Here the judge takes no notice of the widow (presumably a poor woman, and so unable to bribe him) until she makes a nuisance of herself. As in Luke 11: 5ff and 11: 13, Jesus' argument is an *a fortiori* one—how much more will God *avenge his elect.*

This probably refers to those who are persecuted or despised by the world. God would vindicate them, says Jesus. . . . The latter part of 8 seems out of place. It may be a saying of Jesus from another situation or a comment by a Christian preacher.

130. *The parable of the Pharisee and the tax-collector*

Luke 18: 9–14

This is a parable both about prayer and about humility. The men would not enter the Temple building, of course, but stand in the outer court, where groups of people could meet for prayer (cf. Acts 5: 12b) and where the Rabbis discussed with their disciples. Standing was the usual Jewish attitude for prayer.

The Pharisee *prayed with himself* (11); this may mean he prayed silently, to himself, although this seems strange, as he would be more likely to speak his self-congratulations aloud. It may mean he stood by himself and prayed—away from the defiling touch of other people in the courtyard. . . . Jews fasted on Mondays and Thursdays (12). In paying a tenth of all he got (i.e. his whole income) he was really doing more than the Law demanded.

The tax-collector was *justified* not because he was a sinner but because he admitted it and asked for forgiveness. *Justified* means he was declared to be righteous by God. Verse 14b has already occurred in Luke 14: 11.

This parable concludes the non-Markan matter in Luke's travel-narrative. At 18:15 he resumes the Markan narrative (see Sections 93, 94 and 95).

(c) Events at Jericho

131. *The healing of blind Bartimaeus*

Matthew 20: 29–34 Mark 10: 46–52 Luke 18: 35–43

Jericho was the last town through which Jesus would pass on the way to Jerusalem. Then there was a road of sixteen miles to Jerusalem (cf. Luke 10: 30).

Only Mark gives the name of the blind man. *Son of Timaeus* is a Greek translation of Bartimaeus, an Aramaic name. Matthew speaks strangely of two blind men (see also Section 68). . . . The man's cry, *Jesus, son of David*, was a Messianic title. The significance of the story seems to lie in this—the first time Jesus had been called the Messiah in public, according to Mark. Possibly it gave the pilgrims going to Jerusalem for the Passover a hint which they put into action on Palm Sunday. Jesus' question, *What wilt thou that I should do unto thee?* seems to have been asked with the intention of getting the man to state his need. Jesus generally asked for the co-operation of people whom he cured. *Rabboni* (51 in Mark) is a longer form of *Rabbi*, or Teacher.

In Mark this is Jesus' last act of healing.

132. *The meeting with Zacchaeus*

Luke 19: 1–10

This is another instance of the interest of Luke in Jesus' attitude towards outcast people. Here the man was rich, but despised and hated by the people because of his profession.

The statement, *he was little of stature*, has been taken as referring to Jesus. This is grammatically possible, but is unlikely, as the Gospel writers were not concerned to give notes of Jesus' physical appearance. It refers to Zacchaeus. The *sycamore tree* was a fig-mulberry a common wayside tree. In 7 the scene changes to Zacchaeus' house. His declaration in 8 is not a statement of what he usually did but a promise for the immediate future. Both Roman and Jewish law laid down the principle of four-fold restitution for wrong exaction (Exod. 22: 1).

133. *The parable of the pounds*

Luke 19: 11–27

This is similar in many ways to the parable of the talents in Matthew (Section 151). The differences, however, are so numerous that they are best treated separately.

This story seems to be confused by the introduction of the nobleman's *cities* and *enemies* in 14 and 27. It is probable that these are parts of another parable. (They are similar to the insertions into the story of the wedding feast in Matthew—Section 120.) They reflect the relations between Rome and the princes of the East. Josephus says that Herod Archelaus, son of Herod the Great, went to Rome to obtain the kingdom of Judea. The Jews sent an embassage to oppose his claims and the Romans sent him into exile.

If these verses are omitted the parable reads fairly plainly. The point is the reward which follows responsibility faithfully carried out. It may also be a warning to the Jews of Jesus' day, who had been entrusted with a great spiritual treasure—their religion—but had failed to make use of it for the benefit of others. So they were to lose their privileges.

A *pound* was fifty shekels. (Moffatt renders: 'He gave each of them a five-pound note.') The parable seems to end at 24. The exclamation of 25 may be that of Jesus' hearers or may be intended as the remark of the nobleman's friends. The saying in 26 is found also in Mark 4: 25 (and Matt. 13: 12; Luke 8: 18).

Note on miracles

As Mark is probably right in making the healing of Bartimaeus (Section 131) the last miracle of Jesus, this is a convenient place in which to consider the whole question. The miracles of Jesus are often classified as of two types. First there are acts of healing. Many instances are given of these. The diseases and conditions healed by Jesus are mostly functional disorders (as opposed to organic diseases) and many of them are nervous or mental troubles. In the first century these were attributed to demon-possession and there are many cases of exorcism by Jesus. We have noted his methods: faith or confidence on the part of the sufferer or of another person was demanded; Jesus then frequently gave a command, which called forth an effort or the co-operation of the person to be healed.

The others are nature-miracles, of which there are three in the Synoptic Gospels—the stilling of the storm (Section 65), the feeding of the multitude (75 and 80) and the walking on the water (76). In the notes it has been suggested that in each case an explanation is possible which might account for the story as told in the Gospels, without assuming that Jesus had power over the forces of nature.

It should be added that many students of the Gospels consider that this attitude is unsatisfactory and misleading. They prefer to make little or no distinction between the two types of miracles and point out that the miraculous element is woven into the very material of the Gospels. Both the words of Jesus and his acts were 'miraculous'. His life represented the impact of God on the world of men. His work meant the coming of the Kingdom of God (see Luke 11: 20, 17: 20–21). Hence it is only 'natural' that miracles should be part of the story. The Gospels (and the rest of the New Testament as well) set out to be a record of God at work in the world, through Jesus and later through the early disciples. We cannot set a limit to his power and activity.

Nevertheless, miracles do not have for us the same significance as they did for the first-century Christians. We cannot treat them as 'evidences' or proof of divinity and make them the basis of our faith. Those who accept the accounts in the Gospels as they stand would say, not that they believe in Jesus because he worked miracles, but rather that they believe in the miracles because Jesus worked them. Our view must ultimately depend on what we consider to be consonant with his life and character.

V. JESUS IN JERUSALEM

(*a*) Events of Holy Week

134. *The entry into Jerusalem*

Matthew 21: 1–9 Mark 11: 1–11 Luke 19: 28–44

The ovation was probably made by the Galilaean pilgrims to the festival. Jesus himself may not have wished for this. He deliberately chose the ass, as the animal symbolic of peace, used by ordinary people, whereas the horse was the animal representing conquest and worldly might. The popular idea was that the Messiah would come rather in the latter way. The passage in Zechariah 9: 9 (quoted in Matt.) is one of the few places in the Old Testament where a king is thought of as coming to Jerusalem in peace.

Jesus had evidently made arrangements with a friend at Bethany for the ass to be ready and the words *The Lord hath need of him* were a password. Only Matthew quotes the Zechariah passage, although it was probably in the mind of Jesus. Matthew, however, minunderstood the Hebrew. It is an example of poetic parallelism—*the ass*, *the colt*, *the foal of an ass* all mean the same animal. Owing to his desire for a literal fulfilment of Old Testament words in the life of Jesus, Matthew makes Jesus ride on two animals at once!

Hosanna is an Aramaic term meaning literally 'Save us now!' The people may have meant this, appealing to Jesus to act as Messiah and deliver them, or it may indicate a general shout of praise. *Hosanna in the highest* would mean 'Praise in Heaven'. *Blessed is he that cometh in the name of the Lord* is a quotation from

Psalm 118: 26 and was used to greet pilgrims to the Temple for the festival.

Luke adds Jesus' lament over Jerusalem (41–44). It is another warning of the coming siege of the city by the Romans. If only Jerusalem had known the conditions of peace—but now it was too late! *The time of thy visitation* may refer to this visit of Jesus or to the unheeding ignorance of the people of Jerusalem when messengers and prophets from God had visited Judah.

135. *The withered fig-tree*
Matthew 21: 18–22 Mark 11: 12–14, 20–26

In Mark the 'cursing' of the tree and its withering are separated by the events of the day (next section). In Matthew the tree withers immediately. The phrase *it was not the season of figs* (13 in Mark) is an explanation for the sake of Gentile readers. Figs would not be expected on a fig-tree at Passover time.

There are three ways of regarding this story:
(i) As an actual miracle by Jesus. The lesson of the need for faith is then stressed, although there may not seem to be much logical connection. (ii) As an acted parable. The fig-tree represents Judaism (a symbol often employed in the Old Testament for the nation). It was found fruitless and would be destroyed, just as Jesus destroyed the fig-tree. (iii) As a story which has developed in Christian tradition out of a parable. In Luke 13: 6–9 there is a parable about a fig-tree which did not bear fruit (Section 115). As Mark heard it, the parable had become 'hardened' into an incident, in which Jesus destroyed the tree. Possibly there was a dead tree on the road between Bethany and Jerusalem which Jesus pointed out when telling the parable.

The teaching about faith and praying which follows was probably delivered on another occasion (see also Luke 17: 5–6—Section 126). It has been suggested that *this mountain* refers to the hill on which the Temple stood—another hint that Jesus saw that Judaism would be superseded by the work of his disciples. Mark 11: 25–26 (although 26 is omitted in the most trustworthy Greek authorities here) is added by Matthew to the Lord's Prayer (Matthew 6: 14).

136. *The clearing of the Temple court*
Matthew 21: 10–17 Mark 11: 15–19 Luke 19: 45–48

In Mark this takes place the day after the entry into Jerusalem. In Matthew and Luke it appears to follow immediately.

The Temple here means the Court of the Gentiles, which surrounded the inner courts into which only Jews were admitted. In the outer court was a market which supplied worshippers with material for the sacrifices—lambs (for the Passover) and doves and other things for offerings. Jews from other countries were also supplied here with the special Temple money (the *half-shekel*—Matt. 17: 24), which all Jews were required to pay towards the upkeep of the Temple. Roman money was changed into this—at such a rate of exchange that the money-changers made a big profit, as did also the Temple authorities who hired out the courts in this way.

Jesus' action in turning these men out was of course without any official sanction. It was the authority of his indignation which made the people cower. *Carrying a vessel through the Temple* (16 in Mark) probably means that people made a short cut through the court from one part of the city to another, carrying their goods.

. . . Jesus' words are a quotation from Isaiah 56: 7 and Jeremiah 7: 11. Jeremiah had called the Temple of his day *a brigands' cave* (as the words literally mean).

137. *The question of Jesus' authority*
Matthew 21: 23–27 Mark 11: 27–33 Luke 20: 1–8

This is the first of a series of challenges to Jesus on the 'day of controversy'. His opponents' aim was to get him to say something which would discredit him in the eyes of the people and so make him lose his popularity, or else something which would get him into trouble with the Romans.

Priests and scribes and elders represent the three types of people in the Sanhedrin. According to Deuteronomy 18: 15–22, Jewish rulers were expected to test the claims of a prophet, so they were within their rights here. *These things* probably refers to his action in clearing the Temple court and teaching the people as if he were a properly authorized Rabbi.

Jesus did not answer directly, because the question was a trap. *From heaven* means on Jewish lips 'from God'—of divine origin as contrasted with human origin. In the vivid account in Mark the thought of the Jews is left incomplete—the sentence is broken off (32). Matthew (26) and Luke (6) both seek to smooth it out.

138. *The parable of the two sons*
Matthew 21: 28–32

The meaning of the story is that action is pleasing to God, not simply words (cf. the parable of the two foundations—Section 60). The son who actually carried out his father's commands was of course the one who *did* his will. It is another criticism of the Jews of that day, who paid only lip service to God (cf. Mark 7: 6–7). Jesus says that even if they had only observed John's teaching (32), they would be 'on the road to the Kingdom of God'. The phrase *John came in a way of righteousness* appears to mean that John belonged to the Judaistic way of living, but at the same time he foreshadowed a better way.

139. *The parable of the vineyard* (The wicked husbandmen)
Matthew 21: 33–46 Mark 12: 1–12 Luke 20: 9–19

This is one of the few instances where Jesus used a story more like an allegory than a parable. In the Old Testament Israel is frequently spoken of as 'the Lord's vineyard' (e.g. Isa. 5: 2ff). The owner here obviously represents God and the *servants* sent to the vineyard are the prophets. Finally, God's Son was sent, by which the Jews would understand the Messiah. Instead of receiving him, they would kill him, Jesus told his hearers. He publicly announced that the time of judgment on Israel has come. This parable was one of the direct causes of his death, according to the concluding verses in each account.

The details of the owner's action in the vineyard (1 in Mark, 33 in Matt.) need not be pressed; they simply indicate the man's care for his vineyard. The *hedge* or wall would be a protection against wild animals. The *pit* would be under the winepress, to receive the juice. The *tower* would serve as a watchtower against robbers and also as a store-house.

The *stone* in the Old Testament quotation (Ps. 118: 22–23) meant Israel, the nation despised and rejected by other peoples. The early Christians took this as referring to Jesus (Acts 4: 11; 1 Pet. 2:4, 7; Rom. 9:33). In this context it seems to refer to the Messiah, rejected by the people but raised to the place of supreme importance.

140. *The question of tribute to Caesar*
Matthew 22: 15–22 Mark 12: 13–17 Luke 20: 20–26

The aim of Jesus' enemies comes out plainly here. If he answered 'Yes' to their question, he would have lost his popular support; if he said 'No', they could report this to the Romans, who would have arrested him for sedition.

The Herodians are mentioned only here and in Mark 3: 6—both times associated with the Pharisees—a strange alliance. The word *tribute* means in contemporary use a capitation tax. The Romans levied such a tax on the population of Judea from A.D. 6 onwards, when it became part of a Roman province, under a procurator. It was a *denarius* a head—the *penny* here. Judas of Galilee revolted because of the enforcement of this tax. It had to be paid in Roman coins, with the head and inscription of the Emperor on them. The point of Jesus' counter-question, *Whose is this image . . .?* is that the Jews acknowledged the Romans as their overlords, by having such a coin in their possession. According to the ideas of the time, the coins of a ruler actually belonged to him and his authority was considered to hold as far as his coins circulated.

Jesus' final reply was not an evasion but a principle to be applied in circumstances when the problem of allegiance to earthly authority is in question. Jesus did not further define the things of Caesar or the things of God. This was left for the sincere enquirer to think out for himself.

141. *The question of the resurrection*
Matthew 22: 23–33 Mark 12: 18–27 Luke 20: 27–40

The Sadducees did not accept belief in a future resurrection because they held only to the written Law and rejected the oral traditions observed by the Pharisees. They assumed here that Jesus did accept this belief. They came to him with an extreme instance, which was perhaps debated in the Rabbinic schools. The Mosaic law referred to is in Deuteronomy 25: 5–10. They asked for Jesus' judgment, perhaps to make him appear foolish in the presence of the learned debaters.

Jesus' answer seems to argue for the continuance of life after death rather than a resurrection, but perhaps he regarded the greater as including the less, for without survival there could obviously be no resurrection. Jesus showed here a more spiritual idea of the resurrection than many current Jewish beliefs, which tended to be materialistic. The latter part of his argument is: God was spoken of in Moses' time as the God of Abraham, etc. But, although they had lived some centuries before, he is not a God of dead men; therefore they are not dead, but alive.

The phrase *in the place concerning the Bush* (in Mark and Luke) means in the section in Exodus (3: 6) about the burning-bush. It was a popular way of referring to passages in the Old Testament before there were chapter and verse divisions.

Verses 34–35 in Luke are peculiar to his Gospel. *Sons of this age* means people living at the present time; they partake of the nature of this world. *Sons of the resurrection* and *sons of God* mean those who partake of the future age and the nature of God.

142. *The greatest commandment*
Matthew 22: 34–40 Mark 12: 28–34

Luke omits this passage, having previously included a similar incident in 10: 25ff (Section 103).

This was apparently a genuine enquiry, not a catch question. A *scribe* (Mark) or a *lawyer* (Matt.)—the two mean much about the same thing—wanted to know if there was one commandment greater than all the others. There were in the Old Testament 365 prohibitions and 248 positive commands and some of the Rabbis attempted to discriminate between the more and the less important. . . . The first commandment quoted by Jesus is in Deuteronomy 6: 4—a passage which every Jew would know by heart, for it was repeated (and still is) at every synagogue service. The second is in Leviticus 19: 18. . . . Jesus' commendation of the scribe (34 in Mark) is another reminder that Jesus generally thought of the Kingdom of God as something inward.

143. *The question of David's son and warning against the scribes*
Matthew 22: 41–46 Mark 12: 35–40 Luke 20: 41–47

Jesus was here adopting a Rabbinic method of argument. He referred to the popular conception of the Messiah (*the Christ*), that he was a descendant of David. But, he asks, how can the Messiah be David's descendant when David acknowledged him as his lord? His question is unanswered and it is uncertain what his meaning exactly was. It is usually taken that Jesus was arguing that the Messiah was greater than a mere *son of David*, although descended from him. Some think that Jesus was arguing that the Messiah was not descended from David at all. In any case, he wanted his hearers to think out for themselves the real meaning of the Messiahship.

The psalm quoted is 110. It was not written by David but much later and was addressed to a ruler who was priest and king—probably Simon Maccabaeus (about 141 B.C.). In Jesus' time the psalm was regarded as David's and taken as referring to the Messiah. Jesus took the standpoint of his hearers, probably indeed sharing it himself.

The warning against the scribes (38–40 in Mark; 45–47 in Luke) is omitted by Matthew, since he devoted chapter 23 to a denunciation of the scribes and Pharisees (Section 109). The condemnation here is much milder than that. . . . *Long robes* were worn by important people in the East. It is not clear in what way the scribes *devoured widows' houses*. Perhaps it means they acted unworthily when they were made trustees for the estates of widows, or their fees as lawyers used up the widows' money.

144. *The widow's mites*

Mark 12: 41–44 Luke 21: 1–4

The day of controversy closed with a brighter scene. *The treasury* was in the Temple Court of the Women, and held thirteen large chests, trumpet-shaped, into which offerings were put. It would be easy for a rich man to put in a purse of money with ostentation. A *mite* (or *lepton*) was a small brass coin. Two of them made a Roman *quadrans* (a *farthing* here). *All her living* denotes all her means or income.

(*b*) The Apocalyptic Section

145. *Prediction of the destruction of the Temple*
Matthew 24: 1–2 Mark 13: 1–2 Luke 21: 5–6

This is the introduction to a long discourse of Jesus, in which many terms and ideas of current Jewish apocalyptic thought are found. There was a similar passage in Q, found in Luke 17 (Section 128). Matthew has here combined the Markan and Q material to form chapter 24.

Jesus first foretold that the Temple would be utterly destroyed—an event which happened when the Romans sacked Jerusalem in A.D. 70. The Temple was of great size and magnificence. It was built of white marble and the front was covered with plates of gold. Herod the Great began it in 20 B.C., and it was still unfinished at the time of Jesus. Like the Old Testament prophets, Jesus saw the ultimate end of the course the nation was taking.

Sections 146–149 deal with the rest of Mark 13. Much of the material here is found also in the apocalyptic literature—'revelation' books—of the centuries immediately before and after the time of Jesus. In the Old Testament this type is represented by Joel and Daniel and some other passages. The writers sought to 'unveil' the future and they depicted, often in spectacular terms, coming events, which would lead up to a climax of wickedness, to be followed by the victory of God's cause. The early Christians lived in expectation of the 'end of the age' and some of them compiled Christian apocalypses, foretelling the return of Christ (one such is the Book of Revelation in the New Testament).

It has been suggested that such an apocalypse, compiled by a Jewish Christian, has been incorporated here. It is sometimes called 'the Little Apocalypse' and verses 7–8, 14–20 and 24–27 in Mark are regarded as extracts from this. Here the conventional apocalyptic 'signs' are detailed—wars, revolts, famines, desecration, tribulation, wonders in the sky and the coming of the Son of Man. This seems foreign to the outlook of Jesus, for he deprecated the search for such 'signs' (Luke 17: 20–21) and refused himself to give one (Sections 81 and 108).

Genuine sayings of Jesus appear to be included here as well—warnings to the disciples about persecution (9–13) and about misleading claimants (21–23) and exhortations to watch and be on the alert (28–37).

146. *Signs of the end*

Matthew 24: 3–8 <u>Mark 13: 3–8</u> Luke 21: 7–11

The disciples (the three favourites, in Mark) asked a further question: When shall these things be? *These things* refers to the destruction of the Temple, but Matthew adds: *the sign of thy coming and the end of the age* (3). Messianic claimants are referred to in the phrase *Many shall come in my name*, i.e. making use of my name. Then follow the 'signs' (7–8 in Mark) from the apocalypse. *The beginning of travail* (Mark and Matt.) is an allusion to the conception of the tribulations as the 'pangs' which would bring forth the Messiah.

147. *Warnings of trials and tribulation*

Matthew 24: 9–25 <u>Mark 13: 9–23</u> Luke 21: 12–24

The first paragraph is a warning to the disciples similar to that given on other occasions. Verse 11 in

Mark has a parallel in Q (Luke 12: 11–12). Matthew also made use of 9–13 in Mark in the instructions to the twelve disciples in Matthew 10: 17–22.

The word *councils* in Mark (9) is literally 'sanhedrins'. Local synagogues had the right of judging and punishing offenders against the Jewish Law. *For a testimony to them* means: 'You will be able to bear witness even when arrested.' Verse 19 in Luke (often misquoted) means: 'By your endurance you will gain possession of your true souls.'

The second paragraph is thought to be part of the Little Apocalypse. It contains common apocalyptic notes—conflict between good and evil, culminating in the manifestation of an anti-Christ and a great tribulation. *The abomination of desolation* is a quotation from Daniel 11: 31; 12: 11, and 1 Maccabees 1: 54, where it refers to the altar of Zeus which was set up in the Temple at the command of Antiochus Epiphanes in 167 B.C. Swine's flesh was offered on it by the Syrian Greeks. The phrase means 'an appalling horror which produces profanation'. The reference in Mark is apparently deliberately obscure—*standing where he ought not.* Matthew clarifies this—*standing in the holy place*, i.e. the Temple. In Mark it may refer to the desecration to befall the Temple by the presence of Roman armies and their standards in the Temple courts or it may indicate a person who works desolation. Luke changes the phrase to *Jerusalem compassed with armies.*

The aside in Mark and Matthew—*let him that readeth understand* may mean: 'Let the reader of Daniel understand this new application of the passage.' The remainder of the paragraph suggests the circumstances of the Roman invasion of Judea (cf. Luke

17: 31, 34–37—Section 128). The man on the flat roof of his house is to escape by the staircase outside into the street, without first going indoors to pick up his belongings. The phrase about the *shortening of the days* is a reference to the current Jewish idea that the 'great tribulation' would last only a certain time, otherwise everything good would be destroyed. *The elect* are the faithful Messianic remnant who would be saved from the last day.

Mark (21–23) and Matthew (23–25) add a brief warning against false Messiahs. It was a current idea that false teachers and deceivers would herald the conflict between good and evil. The warning against those who might *lead astray* the disciples, however, might well have been given to them by Jesus on more than one occasion.

Matthew inserts (26–28) a paragraph about the appearance of the Son of Man which Luke reproduces in 17: 23–24 and 37 (Section 128).

148. *The coming of the Son of Man*

Matthew 24: 29–31 Mark 13: 24–27 Luke 21: 25–28

Mark is thought to be following the Little Apocalypse here. Matthew expands Mark by adding Old Testament phrases.

The Son of Man was an apocalyptic figure in the time of Jesus. The name went back to Daniel 7: 12–13, where a human figure ('one like a son of man') is taken to represent 'the kingdom of the saints of the Most High', i.e. Israel. Later it was interpreted as an individual—the Son of Man. His appearance in the clouds here is the end of the strife which started with the appearance of the anti-Christ. Signs in the sky were conventional features of apocalyptic (cf. Joel 2: 10; Isa. 13: 10; Ezek. 32: 7–8).

The elect gathered to safety by the angels referred originally in Judaism to the hope that the Jews of the dispersion would return to Palestine for the final establishment of God's Kingdom in Judea. For the readers of Mark it would mean the Christians. *To the uttermost part of the heaven* (27 in Mark) means: from the most distant places of the earth, even from the horizon (cf. 31 in Matt.)

149. *The lesson of the fig-tree and the time of the end*

Matthew 24: 32–36 Mark 13: 28–37 Luke 21: 29–38

The first two verses are a comparison between the way in which men learn from observation of nature and how they should learn from observing these signs. The fig-tree was probably chosen because it was very common in Palestine. . . . *All these things*, it is said here, were to happen in the first century, in that generation. This is no 'long-term' prophecy. But (in Mark and Matt.) Jesus admitted the ignorance of angels and even the Son regarding the exact time of their fulfilment.

Mark and Luke each adds a concluding paragraph about the need for watchfulness, although they are not strictly parallel. Mark 34–35 is a short parable about the return of a householder. The phrases in 35 refer to the four Roman watches of the night. Luke 34–35 has a more generalized warning.

Matthew concludes the chapter (24: 37–51) with matter taken from Q—paralleled in Luke 17: 26–37 (Section 128) and 12: 35–48 (Section 112).

(c) Matthaean Parables

150. *The parable of the ten maidens*
Matthew 25: 1–13

Matthew 25 consists of three parables of judgment and this, with chapter 24, constitutes one of the great discourses of this Gospel.

The general teaching of this parable is the need for watchfulness. The details are not to be pressed. The number *ten* has probably no more significance than as indicating a fair number. Eastern wedding customs are referred to (cf. Mark 2: 19; Matt. 22: 11; Luke 12: 35ff). The *virgins* or maidens were not bridesmaids but maid-servants. They waited to meet the bridegroom in the bride's own house, where he would come in order to fetch her for the wedding. In some manuscripts, however, the words *with the bride* are inserted in verse 1. If this is the true reading, the house was that of the bridegroom, to which he would return with his bride after the wedding.

The *lamps* would of course be oil ones. The foolish maidens had provided oil (8) but not enough, not anticipating such a long wait. Extra oil would be contained in the *vessels* (4) with which the wise maidens had supplied themselves.

It is not stated plainly what it was for which Jesus' hearers had to watch (13). The parable has been generally interpreted to refer to the coming of the Son of Man—addressed first to Jesus' disciples and then to the whole Christian church. C. H. Dodd has suggested that Jesus was referring to the Jews of his own day. They should have been ready to receive the Messiah when he came, but had missed their opportunity.

151. *The parable of the talents*
Matthew 25: 14–30

This is similar to the parable of the pounds in Luke (Section 133). The meaning is the same—the reward which follows responsibility faithfully carried out—but the circumstances differ. The account in Matthew is a more consistent and straight-forward story than Luke's.

A *talent* to us means a gift possessed by someone, but in the Roman world it was a coin—six thousand *denarii*. Its familiar meaning has come from this parable. . . . The praise of the diligent servants (21 and 23) is rendered by Moffatt: 'Come and share your master's feast', for the reference is probably to the Messianic reign, which was pictured as a banquet.

This parable may have been another warning to the Jews. They had been entrusted with a treasure—their religion—but like the slothful servant they had kept it to themselves and had failed to use it for the benefit of others. It would therefore be taken from them and given to others (cf. Matt. 21: 43).

152. *The parable of the judgment*
Matthew 25: 31–46

In an apocalyptic book called The Parables of Enoch there was a picture of the Judgment, when the Son of Man was 'seated on the throne of his glory'. The righteous were rewarded and their oppressors were doomed to torment. If Jesus' hearers knew this parable, they would appreciate the dramatic change which Jesus made. The usual criterion for judgment among the Jews was whether a man had kept the Law faithfully or not. In Jesus' story the test is whether men had fed the hungry, etc., or not done so—whether they had been merciful and generous to their fellows.

Sheep and *goats* (32) represent a conventional division. There was nothing inherently evil about goats or good about sheep! . . . The practice of caring for the sick and the hungry was commended by the Jews. The significant words here are *Ye did it*—or *did it not—unto ME*—the thought that the Son of Man might be in need of such care and that this was the test at the Judgment day. There is some evidence that in the Gospels the term Son of Man means a community—Jesus' *brethren*. . . . The references to the fate of the wicked and the righteous (34, 41 and 46) are conventional Jewish phrases.

(*d*) The Passion Story

153. *The conspiracy of the priests*

Matthew 26: 1–5 Mark 14: 1–2 Luke 22: 1–2

From this point (Sections 153–168) the three Synoptic narratives are parallel, closely so in many places. Matthew follows Mark throughout, with occasional insertions. Luke may have followed Mark, but some scholars think he had his own account which he preferred, only inserting some Markan phrases.

The indication in *After two days was the Passover* seems to mean the Wednesday—two days before the crucifixion. The feast of unleavened bread began at sunset on the day of the Passover festival, but the two were popularly associated together. The Jewish authorities here presumably meant to arrest Jesus and put him out of the way before the actual festival began, in order to avoid *a tumult of the people*, i.e. a riot in his favour. (The chronology of the last few days is obscure and there is divergence between the Synoptic account and that in the Fourth Gospel.)

154. *The anointing at Bethany*
Matthew 26: 6–13 Mark 14: 3–9

Luke omits this, for he has already told of an anointing of Jesus' feet by a sinful woman in Galilee (Luke 7: 36–50—Section 63). This is a different incident, in every particular. The woman in Mark and Matthew is unnamed; the Fourth Gospel puts this incident six days before the Passover and says the woman was named Mary. Later tradition and popular thought have confused all the incidents and all the women concerned.

Simon the leper was presumably healed by this time. He seems to have been a well-known person, although the name was a common Jewish one. The *alabaster cruse* was a phial made of alabaster. The woman broke it by snapping off the neck of the phial. The term *spikenard* in Mark (3) is difficult and probably means pure or genuine nard. Such ointment was greatly valued in the East. *Three hundred denarii* (5) would be a whole year's wage for a working man. The woman must have been wealthy. The expression used by Mark about the attitude of the guests is very strong—'they were very angry against her' (5).

Jesus' reply was startling. He had just been treated as a person of great honour—and started talking about leaving them and being buried! It was usual to anoint bodies after death. Jesus said the woman had anticipated this. . . . The last verse may be a comment by a Christian, who knew that this story was told by preachers, rather than a statement by Jesus.

155. *The treachery of Judas*
Matthew 26: 14–16 Mark 14: 10–11 Luke 22: 3–6

Mark and Luke say that Judas received money, and only Matthew speaks of thirty shekels. Apparently he took this from an Old Testament passage (Zech. 11: 12) which he quotes later on (Matt. 27: 9–10).

It is not clear what Judas offered to disclose to the priests. Some think he told them of the secret of Jesus' messiahship, so giving them a hint about how to challenge him at his trial (Mark 14: 61). Possibly he simply told them that he could lead them to the place where Jesus could be arrested without interference from the crowds.

156. *The Last Supper*
Matthew 26: 17–29 Mark 14: 12–25 Luke 22: 7–27

It is uncertain whether this last meal of Jesus with his disciples was the actual Passover or not. It is so called only in this passage. According to the Fourth Gospel, the Passover was eaten on the day Jesus was crucified, after his death. If this was the Passover meal, the preparations which the disciples were to make would include the provision of a lamb, bitter herbs and unleavened bread, as well as the arrangement of the room. The alternative is to call this meal a Jewish meal of fellowship or *Kiddush*; this may have been later associated with the Passover, of which Jesus and his disciples did not partake that year.

A man bearing a pitcher of water was unusual. Women

generally went to the well. Perhaps the man was a slave or the son of the householder. This is an indication that Jesus had friends in the city, with whom he had made this secret arrangement. He did not want Judas to know, until he had had this last opportunity of fellowship with the twelve. The table-fellowship, now to be broken, would be renewed, Jesus said, in the Kingdom of God (25 in Mark; 29 in Matt.; 16 in Luke.)

Regarding the proceedings at the meal, we may note:

(i) Jesus' indication of the traitor. This is in quite general terms, without mention of the man's name (except in 25 in Matt.). Judas himself would know that Jesus had read his intention. *He that dippeth with me in the dish* is the same as *he that eateth with me*, i.e. one present at the table.

(ii) Jesus' action with the bread and the cup. The host at a Jewish meal used to break a piece of bread and hand it round, after blessing it and giving thanks for it, and similarly with the cup of wine. Here Jesus carried this out while the meal was in progress, adding *This is my body* and *This is my blood.* For the Easterner this would mean: 'This represents me.'

Luke, however, reverses the order, saying that Jesus first took a cup (17), then the bread (19); and he introduces a second cup, *after supper* (20). Verses 19b–20 (*which is given for you . . . poured out for you*) are, however, omitted in some ancient manuscripts and translations (the Western text). They are indeed the same as the words of Paul in 1 Corinthians 11: 25. Many scholars think that they were not written by Luke, but were inserted in some manuscripts by scribes who knew the Pauline account, adding them here in order to 'complete' Luke's narrative.

(iii) The reference to a *covenant*. This recalls the Old Testament conception of religion, the relationship between God and Israel being known as the covenant. The covenant at Sinai was instituted with blood, a sacrifice being offered. Jesus used this metaphor but combined with it other ideas. The words *which is shed for MANY* recall the portrait of the Servant of God in Isaiah 53: 11–12, while the reference to *the new covenant* (20 in Luke, possibly 28 in Matt.) recalls Jeremiah 31: 31–34. . . . The Greek word for *covenant* could also mean a 'will' and was translated into Latin as *testamentum*. Hence it came into early English versions as 'testament', and the book containing the story of the new covenant was called the New Testament.

(iv) The addition in Luke (apart from the doubtful verses 19b–20). He records a quarrel between the disciples even at this table (24–32). Jesus' words are like those in Mark 10: 42–45. *Benefactor* was an actual title (Greek *Euergetes*) used by Eastern potentates in Egypt and Syria. We can see the irony of Jesus here; the true benefactor is one who serves and not one who rules.

157. *Warnings to the disciples and to Peter*

Matthew 26: 30–35 <u>Mark 14: 26–31</u> <u>Luke 22: 28–39</u>

Mark and Matthew are very similar here, but Luke seems to have a different account.

The hymn sung (Mark and Matt.) would be a Psalm. If the meal was the Passover, it would be the Hallel (Ps. 113–118). Peter's boast is typical of the man, as portrayed in the Gospels. Some manuscripts omit *twice* in Mark (30) (and it is not in Matt. or Luke). 'Before cock-crow' may have been Jesus' words, i.e.

before morning broke. Cock-crow was the third Roman watch of the night (cf. Mark 13: 35). If *twice* is included, it may mean one cock answering another, at dawn. Some think it refers to the trumpet-call from the Roman barracks—the *gallicinium.*

The words in 28–30 of Luke are paralleled in Matthew 19: 28. It is a dramatic picture in Luke of Satan 'making a thrust' at Peter and of Jesus' praying for him.

Verses 35–38 in Luke have been explained in various ways. Some think Jesus intended the disciples to fight for him, but this is unlikely in view of his attitude when arrested and his rebuke to the man who did try to defend him (Matt. 26: 52). Others think that he gave a general warning that the disciples must be ready for emergencies. Previously they had no need to worry about such things; now they must be prepared for trials. The disciples misunderstood him to mean that they must buy weapons. A third suggestion is that Jesus was being ironical throughout. If the disciples wanted to defend him by force, they had better get weapons even if it meant selling their clothes! The disciples took him seriously and presented two swords. Jesus closed the topic abruptly with *Enough*!—either a sharp breaking-off of the conversation or else an ironical assent—'That will be enough for your purpose'.

158. *Jesus in Gethsemane*

Matthew 26: 36–56 Mark 14: 32–52 Luke 22: 40–53

Gethsemane was probably a public place. Its name shows that it was an olive orchard. Judas had left the company before this, although the Synoptics do not say when.

Jesus' words, *My soul is sorrowful, even unto death,* mean: 'I suffer an anguish as great as death itself.' In his prayer, Mark gives the Aramaic word he used—*Abba,* meaning 'Father'. Studdert Kennedy commented on Jesus' words, *What thou wilt* . . .: 'The cry in the Garden was an act, not so much of submission, as of aspiration and tremendous resolve . . . "Thy will be done" is not pathetic, it is powerful.' The words *The spirit indeed is willing but the flesh is weak* are often taken to refer to the disciples' case but Jesus may have been referring to himself. He needed the prayers and companionship of his friends.

The men who arrested Jesus were probably members of the Temple police force. These were Levites who kept order in the Temple courts. They were armed with swords and staves, as here. They would be sent under the authority of the Sanhedrin. . . . A kiss was the usual way for a disciple to salute a Rabbi—coming to him, seizing his hand and kissing it. Jesus' remark to Judas (50 in Matt.) may be a question or a command. Perhaps light is thrown on this by the discovery of an ancient drinking cup, with the words inscribed on one side: 'Friend, what are you here for?' and on the other: 'Be merry!' Some think that such an inscription may have been on the cup used at the Last Supper and that Jesus used the words they had all seen that night, as a forcible reminder to Judas of the part he was playing, after having supped with Jesus.

The one who drew his sword is not named. The Fourth Gospel calls him Peter, but the vague phrase in Mark suggests an onlooker. Only Luke records the healing of the servant's ear, while Matthew gives Jesus' rebuke to the impetuous disciple (52–53). . . . The words *that the scriptures might be fulfilled* (49 in Mark,

56 in Matt.) are best taken as a later Christian comment. . . . Only Mark tells of the *certain young man* (51–52). Many people think this is a personal reminiscence and that the young man was Mark himself.

159. *Jesus before the High Priest*
Matthew 26: 57–68 Mark 14: 53–65 Luke 22: 54–55, 63–71

This is the first of Jesus' trials—before the Sanhedrin. (Luke alters *the whole Council* in Mark and Matt. to *the assembly of the elders of the people*, as if it were a kind of Senate, as his Roman readers would understand.) Such a meeting, held at night, was illegal, and some think that this was an informal meeting of members, before the official meeting held at dawn, when sentence was passed.

The accusation made against Jesus was one which would concern Jewish religious laws—that he said he would destroy the Temple (58 in Mark, 61 in Matt.) and build another, an immaterial Temple, in three days (although Matt. speaks of *building it*). It is uncertain what truth lay behind this. Jesus warned the nation of the fate in store for the Jews at the hands of the Romans and foresaw the end of the Temple; there is much evidence in the Gospels of this. Perhaps he said: 'You will destroy this Temple', meaning the Jews would be ultimately responsible, because of their conduct. 'To destroy the Temple' would also mean to bring Judaism to an end and Jesus' enemies seem to have realized what his own disciples did not—that his teaching and influence were incompatible with the continuance of the Jewish legal system and the Temple sacrifices (cf. the accusation made against Stephen in Acts 6: 14).

'To build another in three days' probably means that the requirements of true worship could be satisfied, even without a material Temple, in a very short time. In Jesus' mind there was probably the thought of the invisible Kingdom of God.

This charge was apparently dropped, because the witnesses did not agree. In Jewish law at least two witnesses were necessary to establish a capital charge (Num. 35: 30; Deut. 7: 6; 19: 15).

The challenge of the High Priest was also an illegal proceeding. It is much more dramatic in Mark and Matthew than in Luke. The phrase *the Blessed* (61 in Mark) means God. A confession of Messiahship by Jesus could be interpreted in various ways. It could furnish material for a charge of sedition against the Romans or could form the basis for a charge of blasphemy in Jewish law. The penalty for this was stoning (Lev. 24: 16).

Jesus' reply in Mark (62) was an affirmation—*I am*—but not so definite in Matthew (64) and Luke (70), where the words mean: 'The statement is yours.' The latter part of Jesus' reply (*You shall see the Son of Man. . .*) could not have been meant literally, for the members of the Sanhedrin did not witness this. Some think that Jesus meant that the crucifixion would be a manifestation of his power, through suffering, while others suggest that Jesus was referring to his ultimate triumph after death, saying that the Sanhedrin would realize this. It is possible that these words are an addition by a Christian preacher.

The mocking and smiting of Jesus were indulged in by the attendants and also, apparently, by the Sanhedrin (65 in Mark, 67–68 in Matt.). Luke assigns the insulting of Jesus to the attendants, before the trial began (63–65).

160. *The denials by Peter*

Matthew 26: 69–75 Mark 14: 66–72 Luke 22: 56–62

Peter was in the courtyard, probably below the room where the trial was taking place. Jesus could turn and look at Peter (Luke only—61) because he was now in the courtyard, suffering the insults of the attendants. The accounts do not quite agree who the people were who challenged Peter. He himself would probably be the last person to remember who had actually spoken to him.

The last sentence in Mark (72) is very obscure. The Greek literally means: 'casting upon, he wept.' In addition to the renderings *when he thought thereon, he wept* (Revised Version) and *he began to weep* (margin), it might be translated: 'Casting his cloak over his head, he wept.' A similar phrase is found in contemporary writings as a colloquialism and suggests 'He set to and wept'. Moffatt ('he burst into tears') and the American Revised Standard Version ('he broke down and wept') both well express the general meaning.

161. *The death of Judas*

Matthew 27: 3–10

A different account of the end of Judas is given in Acts 1: 18ff. There Judas is said himself to have bought a field and to have fallen in it, apparently by accident. Hence it was called Akeldama, or 'the field of blood'. In Matthew Judas committed suicide and the priests bought the field, as a burying place for foreigners who died in Jerusalem.

The account in Matthew seems to be based on an Old Testament passage. In Zechariah 11: 4–14 (not

Jeremiah, as Matt. says) the prophet tries to feed the people, after their return from Exile, and to expel their unsatisfactory leaders. But the people are obstinate, so he declares that their covenant with Yahweh is broken. He then asks for his 'hire' and the authorities give him thirty pieces of silver, which he puts into the treasury. *Treasury* was altered in later Hebrew manuscripts (by the omission of one letter) into *potter*. Matthew seems to have known of both readings, for he mentions *the sanctuary* in 5 and a *potter's field* in 10.

162. *Jesus before Pilate*

Matthew 27: 1–2, 11–14   Mark 15: 1–5   Luke 23: 1–5

Mark and Matthew (1) tell of a meeting of the Sanhedrin at dawn, to pass sentence on Jesus and to prepare their case for Pilate. The real trial then began. There is some doubt concerning the actual powers of the Sanhedrin at this time. It is probable that they had no right to try a prisoner on a capital charge, although they might conduct a preliminary examination, and had no power to carry out a death sentence. (Their treatment of Stephen in Acts 7 may have been an outburst of mob violence.)

Pontius Pilate was the sixth of the Roman procurators of Judea, in office from A.D. 26–36. He is said by Philo to have been 'inflexible, merciless and obstinate'. Generally the procurator lived at Caesarea but he would be in Jerusalem to keep an eye on the festival crowds at this time. He probably occupied the Castle of Antonia, a Roman fortress overlooking the Temple.

Luke gives the three charges against Jesus—disturbance of the people, resistance to Roman taxation and the claim to be a king. These were of course political charges, and the reason for his condemnation by the Sanhedrin—blasphemy—was dropped. Luke records Pilate's verdict of 'Not guilty' (4) (see also verses 14 and 22).

163. *Jesus before Herod Antipas*

Luke 23: 6–12

Pilate had control only over Judea. Herod Antipas was tetrarch of Galilee, so Pilate said that he should try the prisoner. For previous interest of Herod in Jesus, see Mark 6: 16 and Luke 13: 31. The *gorgeous apparel* (11) was perhaps a discarded robe of Herod's, put on Jesus to mock his claim to be king.

164. *The condemnation of Jesus by Pilate*

Matthew 27: 15–31 Mark 15: 6–20 Luke 23: 13–25

According to Luke, Pilate made two more attempts to release Jesus (14–15 and 22), proposing to give him a flogging and release him—rough-and-ready Roman justice towards subject races. All three accounts mention the demand for Barabbas—presumably a rebel against the Romans. The crowd who shouted for him were evidently not the Sanhedrin; possibly some partisans of Barabbas arrived to clamour for his release and Pilate saw his opportunity, offering to release Jesus instead. In some manuscripts of Matthew (17) the name of Barabbas is Jesus Barabbas. In this case there is a dramatic choice—'Jesus Barabbas or Jesus called the Christ?'—given to the people.

Only Matthew adds the passages about Pilate's wife and his action in washing his hands (19 and 24–25).

Mark (16–20) and Matthew (27–31) say that Jesus was mocked by the Roman soldiers, after being scourged. This would be while the preparations for the crucifixion were taking place. The *crown of thorns* would be a mocking representation of the laurel wreath, with which victors at the games were adorned and which the Emperor wore on festal occasions. *Hail, king of the Jews* was a parody of the Roman 'Hail, Caesar!' The *purple* (17 in Mark) would be in imitation of the Imperial purple. The *scarlet robe* (28 in Matt.) would be a soldier's cloak.

165. *The crucifixion*

Matthew 27: 32–44 Mark 15: 21–32 Luke 23: 26–43

The person condemned to crucifixion—a form of punishment for slaves and subject races, forbidden for Roman citizens—was first flogged on his bare back. Then he had to carry the wooden cross-piece to the place of execution, where he was nailed (or bound) to it and hauled up so that it fitted across the upright stake in the ground. Then he was left to die—often some days afterwards.

Jesus apparently collapsed through exhaustion and Simon was 'impressed' into the service of the Romans to carry the wood for him. Cyrene was in Libya, North Africa, where there was a Jewish colony. Alexander and Rufus (21 in Mark) were apparently well known to the readers, as Christians. Luke mentions *women of Jerusalem* (27) who followed Jesus. There is evidence that Jewish women used to prepare an opiate to give to condemned men. Jesus again shows that he foresaw the fate to come on Jerusalem (28–30). Verse 31 probably means: 'If they (the Romans) do such things in the time of

Jerusalem's security and comparative peace, what terrible things will they do when stress and strife come?'

Golgotha or Calvary (the Latin rendering) may have been so called because the plot of ground was shaped like a skull, or else because it was the site of a cemetery. The *wine mingled with myrrh* (23 in Mark) was offered by sympathizers to ease the pain or by the women mentioned in Luke. Jesus refused it, to keep his consciousness to the end. . . . The soldiers had the right, according to Roman law, of appropriating Jesus' clothes. They had this as some compensation for their weary duty, for they had to remain on guard until the criminal died, so that his friends should not release him.

The third hour would be 9 a.m. The official account of the criminal (the *titulus*) was affixed to the cross. The Gospels agree that Jesus was crucified as King of the Jews. The robbers were probably bandits or insurgents against the Romans. Luke only has verse 34 and the account of the second malefactor's attitude (39–43). Jesus' reply speaks of *Paradise*. This was an Oriental word, used of the parks of the Persian kings and nobles. By the time of Jesus it had become a general word for a state of happiness. There is no thought here of an intermediate stay in Hades.

166. *The death of Jesus*

Matthew 27: 45–56 <u>Mark 15: 33–41</u> Luke 23: 44–49

All four Gospels agree that Jesus died at 3 p.m. The *darkness over the whole land* (i.e. Judea) is attributed in Luke to an eclipse of the sun, but this would be an impossibility at the time of the full moon. Some have suggested heavy clouds or a storm brought by the south wind, with sand from the desert. Perhaps the darkness is not to be thought of as physical at all; in more than one sense there was 'darkness over the land' of the Jews at this time. Matthew adds other physical events (51b–53) which recall expectations in Old Testament and apocalyptic writings about the Day of the Lord. We need not take them too seriously, especially the story of the resurrection of *the saints*, i.e. pious Israelites and Old Testament heroes.

The cry of Jesus in Mark (34) and Matthew (46) is a quotation from Psalms 22: 1. Some think that Jesus was reciting the whole psalm, which starts with a cry of despair but finishes on a note of confidence and triumph. Perhaps for Jesus this phrase would be the cry of the righteous man in the midst of adversity and does not necessarily represent his own inmost feelings. Some think that Jesus felt he really was deserted not only by men but by God. (The cry is different in 46 of Luke.)

The remark of the bystanders about Elijah reflects the popular idea that this prophet would come before the Messiah (cf. Mark 9: 11). The drink offered to Jesus would be vinegar or sour wine, the ordinary drink of soldiers and working men. The rending of *the veil of the Temple* is probably symbolic. It is a way of saying that the death of Jesus signified the end of Judaism. There were two veils—one between the Holy of Holies and the Holy Place and another between the Holy Place and the outer court. . . . The remark of the centurion in charge of the execution squad is literally *This was a son of God* (Mark and Matt.). For the readers this would mean the Messiah but for him, a pagan, it would mean a manifestation of one of the gods. Luke alters this (47), for the help of his Roman readers.

167. *The burial of Jesus*

Matthew 27: 57–66 Mark 15: 42–47 Luke 23: 50–56

The Romans used to leave the body of a crucified man on the cross, unless some friends of his wanted to bury it. The burial of Jesus would have to take place before 6 p.m. (Friday), for the Sabbath started then and it would not be allowed to remove the body during that day. Arimathaea, where Joseph came from, was a place near Lydda. He was apparently a member of the Sanhedrin—*a councillor* (43 in Mark). He was 'on the look out for the Kingdom of God'.

Mark uses a harsh phrase in 45—*he granted the corpse*—reflecting the brutal or official language of Pilate in 'handing over' the body. The *tomb* was probably a cavern cut out of the solid rock. It was probably intended as a temporary resting-place, until the Sabbath was over. Only Matthew adds the story of the guarding of the tomb (62–66). It has its sequel in 28: 11–15. It is very improbable that the priests would take counsel with Pilate and that they would remember (even if they had heard) predictions of Jesus about a resurrection when his own disciples did not recollect such precise words and were quite unprepared for the appearances of Jesus. The story probably arose in Christian circles as an attempt to refute Jewish accusations that the disciples had stolen the body.

(*e*) The Resurrection

168. *The women's visit to the tomb*

Matthew 28: 1–15 Mark 16: 1–8 Luke 24: 1–12

The Sabbath ended at 6 p.m. on the Saturday. After that the women bought spices (1 in Mark). Luke says they bought them on the Friday afternoon—23: 56. Early on Sunday morning, at dawn, they went to the tomb (2 in Mark). Matthew confuses the two occasions and gives a quite hopeless note of time (1).

The *young man arrayed in a white robe* (5 in Mark) is probably intended to mean an angel. Some think he was one of Jesus' followers, his white clothes denoting a higher class than the disciples. Luke has *two men in dazzling apparel* (4), while Matthew introduces an earthquake, the descent of an angel from heaven and the removing of the stone (2–4).

Mark ends abrupt at verse 8, probably in the middle of a sentence—*for they were afraid*. . . . It might be concluded 'They were afraid of the Jews' or 'They were afraid that they might be thought mad'. Various suggestions have been made—that the original ending of the book, continuing this account and recording an appearance of Jesus to Peter, was lost or that the writer never finished his narrative or completed his book as he intended to do. 'Conclusions' which were attached to the Gospel are found in Section 170.

Matthew adds an appearance to the women (9), while Luke tells of a visit to the tomb by Peter (12). Matthew also gives (11–15) the sequel to his paragraph about the guarding of the tomb in 27: 62–66. The proceedings related here are very improbable (see Section 167).

169. *The appearance in Galilee*
Matthew 28: 16–20

There appear to be present here more than simply the eleven disciples, who *worshipped him*, for *some doubted* (17). Paul mentions an appearance to *more than five hundred brethren at once* (1 Cor. 15: 6) and some think this is the same incident. According to Luke, the apostles did not go to Galilee but remained in Jerusalem and it was in that neighbourhood that Jesus was seen by them (Section 172).

Verses 19–20 are generally taken today to reflect the beliefs and the words of the Church in the writer's own day, rather than those of Jesus himself. It is extremely unlikely that Jesus commissioned his disciples so explicitly to evangelize all nations, for they were reluctant to admit Gentiles into the Church, as we see from Acts. The first disciples confined their work to Jerusalem and the Jews, and the first Gentile conversion took the apostles by surprise. (This is not, of course, to say that the evangelization of the world was not Jesus' intention all along.) It is also not considered that Jesus enjoined baptism into the name of the Trinity, as in verse 19 here. In the early Church baptism was *into the name of Jesus*, as Acts again shows. Such an explicit doctrinal statement as this came later.

The concluding words are *even to the consummation of the age*. The present age was to be brought to an end, according to Jewish thought, in a new and eternal age.

170. *A summary of resurrection appearances*

Mark 16: 9–20

This is one of the later 'Conclusions', appended to the abrupt ending of Mark at 16: 8. It is omitted by the most trustworthy manuscripts and ancient authorities and the style and vocabulary are quite different from the rest of Mark. . . . The contents of the paragraph are based on the resurrection stories in the later Gospels. The first sentence refers to the appearance to

Mary Magdalene in the Fourth Gospel. Verses 12–13 are a reference to the story of the walk to Emmaus (Luke 24: 13–35). Verse 14 is taken from Luke 24: 41–43, and 15 from Matthew 28: 19. Verses 17–18 reflect the experiences of the early Church—exorcisms, speaking with tongues, handling of snakes (cf. Acts 28: 3ff) and healing of the sick.

One Greek manuscript inserts a paragraph at 14 saying that the disciples asked Jesus to 'reveal his righteousness' now, because of the evil in the world and the power of Satan. But Jesus foretold future trials for them but eventual triumph, because of his death.

There was another attempt at a conclusion of Mark found in six Greek manuscripts and other ancient sources. It ran: 'And all that had been commanded them, they (the women) briefly reported to Peter and those who were with him. And after this Jesus himself appeared to them and from the east as far as to the west sent forth through them the sacred and incorruptible proclamation of eternal salvation.'

171. *The walk to Emmaus*

Luke 24: 13–35

Emmaus was about five miles from Jerusalem. Cleopas (18) is not otherwise known and his companion's name is not given. Some have suggested it was his wife. The hopes and yet the hopelessness of the disciples is well reflected in the words in 21.

There must have been something distinctive about the way in which Jesus broke the bread (30)—the usual action of the host at a Jewish meal. The two disciples here had not been present at the Last Supper, so Jesus' action could not have reminded them of that occasion.

The word *saying* in 33 refers grammatically (in most Greek manuscripts) not to *they* (the two) but to *the eleven.* They reported to the two disciples that Peter had seen Jesus. Luke does not say where or when.

172. *An appearance in Jerusalem*

Luke 24: 36–49

This incident seems to follow directly on the previous one, but the occasion may have been later. . . . Luke seems anxious to stress that the appearance of Jesus was not a mere vision (39–43). There is a tendency in his writing to 'materialize' spiritual things and this emphasis here may be because of this.

Verses 44–46 are parallel with 26–27—perhaps a summary by Luke. In 47–49 Luke is thinking of his second volume (Acts), where this 'programme' is carried out.

173. *The ascension at Bethany*

Luke 24: 50–53

This reads as if it took place on the same day as the two preceding incidents. In Acts 1: 3, however, Luke states that Jesus appeared to the disciples for forty days, and then left them. This was at the Mount of Olives (Acts 1: 12)—just before Bethany was reached, on the way out from Jerusalem. Believing in a flat earth, with the heavens above, the disciples naturally thought of Jesus as being *taken up*.

Verses 52–53 form a fitting conclusion to the Gospel.

PART II

The Narrative Portions of the Fourth Gospel

LIST OF SECTIONS

A. *The work of John the Baptist*

John 1: 19–34

For the Synoptic account of John and his preaching, see Sections 12–13.

Here John denies that he is the Messiah or Elijah, who was supposed to come before the Messiah. He is simply *a voice.* The quotation which in Mark and Matthew is applied to John is here put directly into his mouth (23). His statement about one coming after him (26–27) is similar to that given in the Synoptics, except that that here he says this one is *standing in the midst of you.* Bethany beyond Jordan (28) is unknown.

John directly bears witness to Jesus in 29–34. The term *Lamb of God* probably does not refer to the sacrificial system of Judaism, for there was no lamb there which 'took away sins'. The 'sin-offering' was a bullock. A lamb or sheep was slain at the Passover, but this was not strictly a sacrifice. The reference is probably to the *lamb that is led to the slaughter*—the Servant of God—in the Servant Songs in Deutero-Isaiah (Isa. 53: 7).

There is no hint in the Synoptics that John recognized Jesus (except in Matt. 3: 14) and no suggestion that he hailed him in this way. *The Spirit as a dove* which came to Jesus at his baptism (which is not reported) is seen here by John himself and is a 'sign' to him.

One of the themes of the early chapters of this Gospel is the subordination of John to Jesus. The author probably had in mind a sect which venerated John, even placing him above Jesus.

B. *The first disciples*

John 1: 35–51

For the Synoptic account of the call of the first disciples, see Section 15. It is probable in itself that these were followers of John the Baptist, but there is no record in the Synoptics that John directed them to Jesus in this way. It is typical of this Gospel that the Messiahship of Jesus is proclaimed from the beginning, even before Jesus' public ministry (41, 45 and 49).

Who the *other disciple* was, with Andrew (40), we are not told. It may be the same as the one introduced later, under the title of 'the disciple whom Jesus loved'. The nickname of Peter or Cephas is given to Simon also in the Synoptics (Mark 3: 16).

Philip (43ff) is mentioned in the Synoptics as one of the twelve, but Nathanael is a mystery. Some think he was the same as Bartholomew, who is also associated with Philip in the lists of the twelve, but there is no evidence. It is possible he stands simply for the ideal Israelite (47)—a Jew *under the fig-tree*—a metaphor for being 'at home'. The Jew under the Law is called and recognizes Jesus; he is promised visions and spiritual experiences (51). Some have thought there is a reference here to Paul.

C. *The marriage at Cana*

John 2: 1–11

This is the first of seven 'signs' in the Gospel—the term given here to Jesus' miracles. Each of them is intended to bring forth 'belief'. This is said to have been for the benefit of the disciples and to show the 'glory' of Jesus (11).

The reply of Jesus to his mother (4) is not so harsh in the Greek as it sounds in English. *Woman* was a respectful term of address. Jesus puts her off with a mild rebuff. The idea of Jesus' *hour*—the time of his glorification—is a favourite one in this book. . . . The *firkin* (6) is about nine gallons, so there would be between a hundred and six and a hundred and sixty-two gallons of water here.

This story is quite unlike the Synoptic works of Jesus and as a miracle it seems to have no ethical value or spiritual purpose. Some, however. are prepared to take it as a record of literal fact, showing Jesus' participation in the joyous occasions of life. Others suggest that this is an instance of the symbolism of this writer. The historical basis may have been some wedding feast which 'went off well' because of Jesus' presence, but the writer uses this to give his own teaching to his readers. The water in the pots stands for Judaism—*set there after the Jews' manner of purifying* (6). Under the influence of Jesus it becomes the richest wine. The huge quantity of water and the phrase *up to the brim* (7) emphasize the greatness of the transformation. So the author pointed out how the tasteless water of the Jewish religion had become the wine of Christianity.

D. *The Passover at Jerusalem*

John 2: 12–25

See Section 136 for the Synoptic account of the clearing of the Temple court. Only here is Jesus said to have made *a scourge of cords* (15)—probably a light whip from the rushes which lay on the ground for the cattle. Jesus' statement to those who were buying and selling is also different (16).

Destroy this Temple . . . (19) reminds us of the charge made against Jesus at his trial (Mark 14: 58). The statement of Jesus may have been 'You will destroy this Temple', i.e. the Jews would be responsible for its destruction, although this was actually carried out by the Romans. We have evidence from the other Gospels that Jesus foresaw the end of Judaism. The requirements of true worship—not a visible Temple but the invisible Kingdom of God—could be furnished *in three days*—an Eastern idiom for a very short time. The comment in 21 is that of the author and seems to miss the point.

The knowledge of men shown by Jesus (24–25) is one of the characteristics of the divine Logos, as this writer thinks of Jesus.

In the Synoptics this incident occurs on the last visit to Jerusalem, just before the crucifixion. There are three possibilities:

(i) That it happened twice. It is, however, very unlikely that the Jewish authorities would have allowed this.

(ii) That the Fourth Gospel is right. The Synoptics relate only one visit to Jerusalem, so they had to put it there.

(iii) That the Synoptics are right. It was the climax of Jesus' relations with the authorities and was the reason for the opposition of the priests to him. This writer may have put it at the beginning to make Jesus challenge the system of Judaism from the very start of his ministry.

E. *The interview with Nicodemus*

John 3: 1–10

Nicodemus is not mentioned in the New Testament apart from this Gospel (see also John 19: 39).

The only occurrence of the term *Kingdom of God* in John is here (3, 5). In the Synoptics it is the main theme of Jesus' preaching and teaching. *Eternal life* (15, 16)—a frequent term in this book—is apparently regarded as its equivalent. . . . Being *born anew* (or *from above*) is an Old Testament thought, applied to the rebirth of the nation (Ezek. 36: 25–27); hence the query of Jesus in 10. But there is a Greek background as well and the readers would be familiar with such terms and ideas from the mystery-religions. These claimed to give their adherents a 'rebirth into eternity'. Here it is John's way of stating the Synoptic saying about 'turning and becoming as little children'. To be born anew means to start life afresh, at the beginning—as a child.

From 11 onwards the interview becomes a monologue and fades into the comments of the writer.

F. *The woman of Samaria*

John 4: 1–42

In the Synoptics Jesus begins to preach after the imprisonment of John the Baptist (Mark 1: 14), but here (1) they work alongside for a time (cf. 3: 21–24).

Jews generally avoided Samaria when travelling from Judea to Galilee (see 4). The reference to *Jacob's well* in 5 is to Genesis 33: 19 and 48: 22. The bones of Joseph were said to have been buried here later (Josh. 24: 32).

Noon (6) was an unusual hour to draw water, in the

heat of the day. The woman's character explains why she came at this time, alone. Her remark (19) recalls the 'insight' characteristic of Old Testament prophets and seers. She perceived that Jesus read her character. *This mountain* (20) is Mount Gerizim. The Samaritans, after being refused permission to help in rebuilding the Jerusalem Temple after the return from Exile, built a rival one in Samaria. It was destroyed by the Jewish king, John Hyrcanus, in 130 B.C.

The phrase in 24 should be *God is spirit*. It is not a definition of God but a description of his nature. . . . As elsewhere in John, the Messiahship of Jesus is openly proclaimed from the start (26). The disciples were surprised (27) because it was not 'the thing' for a Jewish man to speak with a woman in public. . . . There may be a proverbial saying in 35, inculcating patience for the harvest after the period of sowing—'Four months before harvest'. This may be an indication that the time here was December or January. Jesus warns the disciples against impatience—yet the harvest (in Samaria) is present. John is probably thinking (in 37–38) of the preachers (the reapers) of his own generation.

G. *The healing of the nobleman's son*

John 4: 46–54

This resembles in some ways the story of the centurion's servant (Section 61). Some scholars think it is the same incident, told in this author's own way. It is specified as *the second sign* (54) (cf. 2: 11) and brings forth belief in one outside the circle of the disciples.

H. *The healing of the lame man at Jerusalem*

John 5: 1–18

Both the occasion (1) and the place (2) are uncertain. The word for *gate* is not in the Greek and the phrase can mean 'the sheep gate' or 'the sheep market' or 'the sheep pool'. Bethesda should probably be Bethzatha, in the north of Jerusalem.

Later and inferior manuscripts added a statement (4) about an angel who came down to stir the water. The pool probably had healing properties, which were present when the spring bubbled up. . . . The command to the man is like that in Mark 2: 11. The *bed* would be a pallet or light mat. It was illegal to carry a load on the Sabbath (10), as that constituted work. Jesus' reply to the charge of breaking the Sabbath is different from that in the Synoptics (Mark 2: 27–28 and 3: 4).

I. *The feeding of the five thousand*

John 6: 1–15

Cf. Section 75. John adds to the Synoptic account the time of the incident (4), the mention of Philip (5), the introduction of a boy (9) and the reaction of the people (14–15). He also makes the incident the occasion for teaching by Jesus and retells it with this in view. It is one of the *signs* (14), which convinces *the people.*

J. *The journey across the lake*

John 6: 16–21

Cf. Section 76. John adds that the disciples *were willing to receive Jesus into the boat* (21) but omits the statement in Mark that *he would have passed them by.* He also adds that the boat immediately came to the land. This suggests the disciples were nearer the shore than they had supposed.

K. *The judgment of the adulteress*

John 8: 1–11

Although this is in the English versions, it is certain that it is not part of the Fourth Gospel. It is omitted in all the early and most trustworthy authorities—Greek manuscripts and translations. The vocabulary and style are quite unlike the rest of the book. It is more like a Synoptic narrative and one manuscript puts it in Luke. Its contents, however, show it is a genuine story about Jesus.

The Old Testament said that people committing adultery should be put to death, but these severe laws were rarely enforced. The case here may have been a trap for Jesus. If he said the woman was to be stoned, he would get into trouble with the Romans. If he let her off, he could be charged with disregard for the Jewish Law. Jesus' reply (7) is an illustration of *Judge not. . .* (Matt. 7: 1ff).

L. *The healing of the man born blind*

John 9: 1–41

This story is vividly told and there is depicted the gradual development in the reponse of the man and his belief in Jesus (see 11, 17, 25, 33 and 38) and, on the other side, the growing opposition of the Jews.

The popular idea was that illness and affliction were the result of sin. The disciples argued that since the man was *born* blind, it must have been his parents' sin (2–3). Jesus' reply seems to state that he was blind in order that Jesus might proclaim the works of God, by healing him. This seems very hard. The suggestion has, however, been made, that the difficulty disappears if we punctuate the sentence differently (in early Greek manuscripts there were no marks of punctuation). If we put a stop after *parents* and a comma after *him*, Jesus abruptly answers the disciples' speculation and continues: 'In order that God's work may be made plain, we must work . . .'—and proceeds to heal the man.

The double meaning often found in John is exemplified in 34. *They cast him out* means the Pharisees expelled him from their presence. But the writer was thinking of the conduct of the Jews of his own day and their attitude towards people who became Christians. They excommunicated them, forbidding them to worship in the synagogue.

M. *The raising of Lazarus from the dead*
John 11: 1–46

In John this incident is the immediate cause of the plot to arrest Jesus and kill him. In the Synoptics the cause is the clearing of the Temple court and Jesus' teaching; no account is given of Lazarus at all.

Mary and Martha lived in *a certain village* in Luke 10: 38ff—not apparently Bethany, but between Galilee and Jericho. . . . The 'glorification' of Jesus (4) is one of the themes in this Gospel. Jesus is here very human (5) but is nevertheless the self-determined Logos, making his own programme (6). His absence (15) and even his prayer (42) are intended to inculcate 'belief'.

It was a Jewish idea that the soul stayed near the body for three days after death; then it departed, since the body began to decay (17). The writer's teaching about eschatology ('the last things') comes out in 23–26. Martha represents the conventional outlook of the Jews —belief in a resurrection *at the last day*. Jesus had apparently referred to this (23) but then emphasized that the resurrection was a present reality (25–26).

There are three views of this story:

(i) That John narrates an historical incident. He makes use of it to introduce his teaching, his favourite terms and ideas.

(ii) That there is an historical basis, which has been elaborated in characteristic fashion to bring out the themes of life and death, just as the story of the man born blind (Section L) brings out the opposition of light and darkness.

(iii) That the story has simply a symbolic meaning. It may be built up from hints in the Synoptic narratives —the mention of Martha and Mary in Luke 10 and the parable about Lazarus in Luke 16: 19ff. In the parable Lazarus was not allowed to return from the dead, to convince the brothers of the rich man. John says that when Lazarus did return, the Jews were still unconvinced (cf. Luke 16: 31).

N. *The anointing at Bethany*

John 12: 1–8

For Synoptic stories of anointing, see Sections 63 and 154. The latter case seems to be the basis of this incident; but the woman is named as Mary and the house is Martha's. Jesus' feet are anointed, not his head—a detail from Luke 7.

Spikenard (3) probably means 'genuine nard'—an expensive ointment. *Three hundred denarii* (5) would be a year's wages. Verse 7 may be: 'Let her alone in order that she may keep it' or, 'Allow her to keep it'. But Mary had already used the ointment and could not keep it, unless it had not all been used. It has been suggested that the Greek is a misunderstanding of an Aramaic statement and should read: 'Let her alone. Should she keep it for the day of my burial?'

O. *The entry into Jerusalem*

John 12: 12–19

Cf. Section 134. Only John mentions the *palms* (13) which have given this day its distinctive name. He also, as Matthew, quotes the passage from Zechariah 9: 9.

P. *The washing of the disciples' feet*

John 13: 1–11

John has no account of the Last Supper as told in the Synoptic Gospels (Section 156). He substitutes this story and the discourses of Jesus in chapters 13–17.

Before the feast of the Passover (1) is stressed (cf. 18: 28 and 19: 14). In the Synoptics this meal is the Passover supper. Jesus' action (4–5) was that of a slave, generally performed at the beginning of a meal, when the guests entered the room. They would recline on couches round the table, with their feet projecting behind. So a slave could go quietly round and bathe their hot and dusty feet.

Q. *The arrest of Jesus*

John 18: 1–11

Cf. Section 158. John omits the name Gethsemane and the salutation of Judas to Jesus. He makes Jesus give himself up willingly (5, 8). He mentions a *cohort* of soldiers (3) and the names of Peter and Malchus (10–11). The soldiers were not necessarily Roman ones; they may have been the Jewish police.

R. *The Jewish trial of Jesus*

John 18: 12–27

Cf. Section 159. Jesus here appears before Annas, the High Priest who had been deposed by the Romans, and then before Caiaphas, his son-in-law. No definite charge is made against him here and no statement of his actual condemnation.

Another disciple is introduced (15), who may be the same as 'the disciple whom Jesus loved'. Many suggestions have been made as to his identity—that he was Nicodemus, Joseph of Arimathaea, Mark, Lazarus, John the apostle or even Judas Iscariot. *Known to the High Priest* does not necessarily mean kinship or relationship; it may be translated 'an acquaintance' or 'a familiar friend'. The unnamed disciple was evidently an important person in Jerusalem.

S. *The trial before Pilate*

John 18: 28–19: 16

Cf. Sections 162 and 164. The accusation made against Jesus here is the vague one that he must have been an evildoer (30), but Pilate asks Jesus the same question as in the Synoptic accounts (33). In the interview between Pilate and Jesus (33–38) some leading ideas of this Gospel are brought out and discussed—*the world, truth, witness.*

Pilate's acquittal of Jesus is emphasized in 19: 1–6 (as in Luke 23). Verse 7 has a religious meaning, but there may be a suggestion of political offence as well. The Emperor was called *a son of God* (*divi filius*) as one of his titles, so a charge of treason may be hinted at here. Pilate's fear may have been due to that or may have been superstition. . . . John emphasizes again that this all took place before the Passover (18: 28 and 19: 14).

T. *The crucifixion and burial of Jesus*
John 19: 17–37

Cf. Sections 165–167. John adds to the Synoptic accounts and sometimes conflicts with them, e.g. in the statement that Jesus carried his own cross (17) (cf. Mark 15: 21). The title over the cross (19) seems to be a conflation of the Synoptic versions. The references to the three languages (20), the seamless robe (23–24), and the water and blood (34) are plainly symbolic.

The 'beloved disciple' here has his home in Jerusalem (26). Some think he represents here an ideal figure, rather than an actual person. Only John mentions the spear-thrust in Jesus' side (31–34). It was the practice of the Romans to break the legs of a crucified criminal with a small mallet, if they wished to hasten death. Verse 35 is as awkward in the Greek as in the English. *He that hath seen* and *borne witness* is probably not the author, but the 'witness' behind his account. Then who is *he*, who *knoweth that he saith true*? It has been held that he is: (i) God; (ii) Christ; (iii) the 'witness'; (iv) the author; (v) the editor of the Gospel, who may have inserted this verse.

Only John says it was *a garden* where the tomb was (41). He also adds Nicodemus to the Synoptic mention of Joseph of Arimathaea (39).

U. *The resurrection appearances*

John 20: 1–29

There are four accounts here: (i) the finding of the empty tomb (1–10); (ii) the appearance to Mary Magdalene (11–18); (iii) the appearance to the disciples (19–25); (iv) another appearance, with Thomas present (26–29).

Verses 1–10: Cf. the Synoptic story in Section 168. Here Mary finds the stone removed from the mouth of the tomb, Peter and another disciple find the tomb empty and later Mary sees two angels (12–13).

Verses 11–18: This is only in John. *Touch me not* (17) is literally 'Do not cling to me'. The reason for this command does not seem logical. By an emendation in the Greek we may read: 'Do not fear.' The author apparently thinks of the ascension as taking place between this time and the appearances to the disciples later on.

Verses 19–25: Only John mentions the *fear of the Jews*. Verses 19–21 seem to reflect Luke 24: 36–49. But here the Spirit is given to the disciples immediately, without their waiting in Jerusalem until Pentecost.

Verses 26–29: John does not say Thomas did accept Jesus' invitation to feel him. The latter part of 29 plainly has the readers of the Gospel in mind—the second generation of Christians.

V. *A resurrection appearance in Galilee*

John 21: 1–23

The Gospel comes to a fitting conclusion in 20:30–31. This chapter is obviously an appendix, although it is not agreed whether it was added by the writer himself or by a later disciple.

The journey of the disciples back to Galilee agrees with Matthew 28:16. The story of the catch of fish is like Luke 5: 1ff (Section 16). The number of fish caught is a symbolic detail (11); there were reckoned to be a hundred and fifty-three species of fish in the sea. The number stands for humanity complete, the nations of the world.

Peter is commissioned three times (15–23), as he had denied Jesus three times. There are different Greek words used for *love* in 7 and 8 and for *sheep* and *lambs* and for *feed* and *tend*. There is no subtle distinction between the pairs of words; they are used simply for the sake of variety. The two words for *love*, for instance, were used indiscriminately in the New Testament and the Hellenistic world.

The 'beloved disciple' seems to have been dead by the time 20–23 were written. His death caused a difficulty to the Christians, in view of the rumour that he would not die before the return of Christ. This paragraph was intended to put this in its proper perspective.

BOOKS FOR FURTHER STUDY

Books marked with an asterisk are of a more advanced nature. Books and commentaries which are based on the Greek text of the Gospels are not included in this list.

The composition and characteristics of the Gospels:

*M. Dibelius: *From Tradition to Gospel.*
H. A. Guy: *A Critical Introduction to the Gospels.*
*B. H. Streeter: *The Four Gospels.*
R. V. G. Tasker: *The Nature and Purpose of the Gospels.*
*V. Taylor: *The Formation of the Gospel Tradition.*
V. Taylor: *The Gospels: A Short Introduction.*
D. F. Wilson: *The Gospel Sources.*
A. Barr: *A Diagram of Synoptic Relations.*

The contents of the Gospels:

C. H. Dodd: *The Parables of the Kingdom.*
A. M. Hunter: *The Words and Works of Jesus.*
H. Martin: *The Parables of the Gospels.*
T. W. Manson: *The Sayings of Jesus.*
*T. W. Manson: *The Teaching of Jesus.*
*B. T. D. Smith: *The Parables of the Synoptic Gospels.*
H. A. Guy: *The Study of the Gospels.*

Books on separate Gospels:

The Clarendon Bible volumes: *St. Mark* (Blunt); *St. Matthew* (Green); *St. Luke* (Balmforth); *St. John* (Rattey).

*The Moffat New Testament Commentary volumes: *Mark* (Branscomb); *Matthew* (Robinson); *Luke* (Manson); *John* (Macgregor).

The Torch Commentary volumes: *St. Mark* (Hunter); *St. Matthew* (Cox); *St. Luke* (Browning); *St. John* (Richardson).

The Cambridge Bible Commentary: *Matthew* (Argyle); *Mark* (Moule); *Luke* (Tinsley); *John* (Hunter).

The Penguin Gospels: *Mark* (Nineham); *Matthew* (Felton); *Luke* (Caird); *John* (Marsh).

*A. E. J. Rawlinson: *The Gospel According to St. Mark.*

W. F. Howard: *Christianity According to St. John.*

*E. F. Scott: *The Fourth Gospel.*

H. A. Guy: *The Origin of the Gospel of Mark.*

*C. H. Dodd: *The Interpretation of the Fourth Gospel.*

V. Taylor: *Behind the Third Gospel.*

Index of Passages in the Synoptic Gospel

(The numbers relate to the sections)

Index to Parables

Index to Chief Events, People and Places